SEO

FOR BLOGGERS

HOW TO RANK YOUR BLOG POSTS AT
THE TOP OF GOOGLE'S SEARCH
RESULTS

R.L. Adams

From *The SEO Series*

by

R.L. Adams

- *SEO Simplified – Learn Search Engine Optimization Strategies and Principles for Beginners*

- *SEO Black Book – A Guide to the Industry's Secrets*

- *SEO White Book – Unlock the Power of Organic Search Engine Optimization*

- *SEO for Bloggers – Learn How to Rank your Blog Posts at the Top of Google's Search Results*

SEO FOR BLOGGERS

All Rights Reserved

FTC & Legal Notices

The Author was complete as possible in the creation of this book. The contents within are accurate and up to date at the time of writing however the Author accepts that due to the rapidly changing nature of the Internet some information may not be fully up to the date at the time of reading. Whilst all attempts have been made to verify information provided in this publication, the Author assumes no responsibility for errors, omissions, or contrary interpretation of the subject matter herein. Any perceived slights of specific people or organizations are unintentional. There are affiliate links to products and services in this guide. The author will get paid if you purchase some of the products or services recommended as links within the content of this book. The author was not prepaid to recommend any of the products or services listed in this book but will generate an income, whether fixed, or recurring, on some of the links listed in this book.

CONTENTS

WHO THIS BOOK IS FOR

I've designed and written this book for anyone that's looking to enhance his or her knowledge of the SEO trade from a blogging perspective. If you're a blogger, or you're thinking about entering the blogosphere, you have to understand just what it takes to rank your blog's articles on Google's search results pages. However I think that pretty much goes without saying, and without this knowledge you could be spinning your wheels for years, wondering why your blog's traffic is languishing. Also, I've written this book with the general premise that you're using Wordpress for your blogging platform. And although the concepts and principles that I teach in this book can be applied to any blog, or Website for that matter, the specific instructions and recommendations have been written specifically for Wordpress.

Since the potential for income generated by your blog is a direct result of the amount of Web traffic you're able to produce with your blog articles, it goes without saying that the greater your knowledge in the field of SEO, the greater your potential for income in blogging. But SEO doesn't come easy and if you've had any brush-ins with it then you probably already know that SEO takes a lot of work and understanding. For most, it takes years to develop the technical know-how and skillset that I convey in the pages of this book. But that's because the resources that are available for SEO are mostly either outdated, or don't provide enough information at all to truly master the trade. But that won't happen here. My goal in this book is to convey you to my decade-long knowledge and know-how in the field.

But either way you look at it, SEO is hard work, even when you know and understand all of its nuances. So, you'll need to keep in mind that you have to stick to your efforts because SEO authority won't happen overnight. Even with all of the information that I've presented in this book, SEO will still takes a concerted daily effort on your part. It takes daily efforts of dropping links, posting on forums, commenting on blog posts, doing guest blogging, sharing on social media sites, and the dozens of other different activities involved in SEO. But as a blogger, you're probably used to hard work and I would imagine that you wouldn't shy away from a little challenge. And as you'll come to find, over time as you do a little bit each and every single day, you will see your blog traffic begin to skyrocket.

So whether you're brand new to the blogging industry, or you have a little bit of blogging behind your belt, you will find the information in this *SEO for Bloggers* book highly useful, practical and very current and up to date. You will come to find that by implementing the strategies that I discuss in the pages of this book, over time, you'll find your blog ranking at the top of Google's search results. However, to get there you must begin building Google's trust. We'll take a look at all the different components involved with creating trust for a blog on the Internet today. We'll also take a look at just how these different components affects your blogs potential to rank on Google.

If you've already done some SEO work, and you've done the wrong kind of work, you may have hurt your blog's chances for rankings rather than helped it. You may not see the effects of that hurt until Google runs its next algorithm update, but it'll happen. It's the unfortunate nature of the Google search environment today, which is a product of so much abuse by a small group of individuals that Google had to make some drastic changes. But, as you'll come to find, as long as you stick to a strategy of producing high quality content that is well researched, your blog will begin to soar in the rankings. So, whether you have no experience with SEO, or you have some behind your belt, strap in and prepare to get your hands dirty. This is going to take some work.

INTRODUCTION

I've been blogging for a really long time. Ever since before the current modern day blog platforms were released in fact. I still remember some of the crude early iterations of the Wordpress platform, and it sure has changed and evolved ever since those early days. But blogging itself has grown tremendously in that period of time as well. It went from a simple novelty to something so mainstream that it has taken the Internet by storm. Everyone these days want to be a blogger. Some want to do it for the sheer enjoyment of writing and publishing their works for the world to see, but most want to do it for one simple reason: extra income. And over the past several years, what started out as a hobby for most folks, has evolved into a full-time job for some. All of this has made the allure of blogging much more attractive to the millions of people intrigued by the trade each year.

However, like anything else in this world, blogging takes some serious and concerted effort and technical know-how. Some people are drawn to the blogosphere when they hear of these rags-to-riches stories of bloggers getting ridiculously wealthy. There's even been an outcropping of network marketing sites dedicated to preying on this get rich quick scheme of making money overnight by blogging. But making money by blogging isn't as simple as most people think because it requires some serious technical know-how. Aside from being able to write very well written, well-researched and informative articles, a blogger's technical knowledge of the Web and positioning their articles on Google's SERPs, is paramount to his or her success.

If you're thinking about becoming a blogger, or you've already entered the blogging industry, then you most likely understand just how difficult it is to rank your blog posts on Google. This is probably one of the most specific skillsets that are required in this trade in order to make money. This is because to make money with a blog you need traffic. And to get Web traffic you need to understand SEO, or search engine optimization. If you can't rank your articles high on Google, then you will wind up with a great blog, but no one to visit it. If you can't rank on Google, then you won't have the Web traffic, which will help to generate you income from your Blog.

You see, bloggers make money based on their Web traffic. It's the Web traffic to the blog that allows ads and affiliate links to be displayed and potentially clicked on in order for the blog owner to generate income. Some income streams require the simple display of advertisements on the blog's pages such as Google's AdSense. Other income streams require clicks, and still others require sales from affiliate links. But none of that can happen without Web traffic, and a lot of Web traffic. That's because it's all a play on the numbers. The more visitors a blog has, the more of a likelihood that those visitors will turn into buyers.

Since Web traffic plays such a large role in the success

of a blog it's important to understand, in finite detail, SEO and how to craft your articles in a way that will be highly optimized for Google's search engine results pages (also known as SERPs). When you can understand SEO, and all the nuances involved in ranking your blog's articles on Google's SERPs, you can watch your Web traffic increase exponentially. But it's not going to happen overnight. SEO takes some real down and gritty work that will involve daily action items required on your part in order to increase the overall Web presence of your blog.

As time goes on, and you stick to writing your articles form an SEO perspective, and each article gains in visibility on Google, your overall blog's authority will rise. Authority refers to the importance that a Website has on the Internet. And one of the strategies involved in ranking your blog articles high on Google's SERPs will be to leverage existing authority sites to help improve the overall ranking of your own site. But this needs to happen over time, because Google has caught on to many of the schemes employed by clever SEO specialists.

Google has caught on because at a time not too long ago (a few years back), the Internet became saturated with Web spammers that were dominating Google's SERPs. They were able to employ some stealth-like SEO techniques that saw them begin to monopolize SERPs for any keyword they chose. Google decided to fight back, and as a result it instituted some new rules. These rules are the confines of the Web that you must now work in. If you want your blog to succeed you have to both understand these rules and how they affect you, as well as learn to employ a new set of tactics that will help you play by the rules while still providing the maximum benefit possible for your blog's rankings.

In this book, I will help you understand how to SEO your blog and provide you with the inherent knowledge and know-how to rank your blog posts on Google's SERPs. This book is the fourth SEO book in *The SEO Series* that I've released, and it is a repository of knowledge that will get you current with all of the SEO rules in ranking your blog posts today. You will be hard pressed to find another resource with the style and breadth of information included in this book for ranking your blog posts with SEO today. This book is the synergy of the first three books on SEO in the series, but with a laser-focused target of being designed specifically for bloggers.

In 2012 it was reported that were there 59.4 million Wordpress blogs, 87.8 million Tumblr blogs, and a combined Webpage view of those blogs upwards of 21.3 billion times over. That number is staggering, but to compete in this very saturated blogosphere marketplace you have to have the knowledge and know-how to rank. This book will give you that knowledge and know how. If you can commit to reading the pages of this book and doing a little bit each and every single day, you will be well on your way to having a top blog, no matter what industry that may be in.

1
AN SEO OVERVIEW

To truly understand SEO, you have to understand the state of the Internet today, because a lot has changed. The changes that have come about have been very utilitarian in the eyes of Google, and they will affect your ability to rank your blog today, so it's important to have a brief overview of them. You see, since 2011 Google has begun introducing changes to its algorithm. The algorithm is the formula that ranks Websites on Google's SERPs. Now, the exact algorithm is kept a secret, because that would defeat the whole purpose of having an organic search engine. Google wants the search results to be natural and organic, meaning it doesn't want people trying to cheat their way to the top, which is exactly what was happening in the past.

Google was always an organic search engine, but as time wore on, SEO specialists began uncovering secret methods and techniques for pushing and prodding their way to the top of Google's SERPs. They used something today known as Black-Hat SEO techniques. Black-Hat SEO techniques are described as those that directly violate Google's Webmaster guidelines. These include practices such as keyword stuffing, content cloaking, and participating in link schemes just to name a few. In stark contrast to Black-Hat SEO is White-Hat SEO, the acceptable methods and techniques that comply with Google's Webmaster Guidelines. You can find a complete list of Google's Webmaster Guidelines at the following URL: http://bit.ly/webmstrguidelines.

As time wore on and Google realized what was going on, it began to formulate its methods for fighting back. Google needed to take back control of the Web, and it needed to do it fast. Google did this by releasing a number of algorithm updates. Namely it released three major updates:

- **Google Panda** – First released in February of 2011, the Google Panda was aimed at punishing low-quality content, duplicate content sites, and poor user experiences, while promoting high quality, unique-content sites. The update was created by Google using a very sophisticated type of machine-learned algorithm that that utilized thousands of users' rankings for sites that they considered high quality, and those they considered low quality. The algorithm then learned and scaled this method, and went about adjusting its rankings across the board.

- **Google Penguin** – This was a more severe update released by Google. First announced in April of 2012, the Google Penguin was the evolution of the Google Panda. The Panda mainly focused its efforts on the user experience, which included content but also the content that appeared above the Website fold. The Website fold is where the Webpage generally gets cut off on most browsers before having to scroll. But the Penguin went above and beyond the Panda, and this is where Google introduced demotion for what they considered Black-Hat SEO practices. This would include keyword stuffing, content cloaking, and the participation in link schemes.

- **Exact-Match Domains** – This update, released in September of 2012, targeted low-quality Websites that were exact match domains. An exact-match domain is when the domain name is the same as the targeted keyword. For example, iPhone6Rumors.com would be an exact-match domain name for the keyword "iPhone 6 Rumors." This algorithm update ventured out to demote exact-match domains that had low-quality content. This is not to say that this technique of creating a Website on an exact-match domain doesn't work, you just have to ensure that if you go down this route now that the domain name has quality content and good linking authority.

These updates have ranged from mild to severe and have really been targeted at punishing certain sites and Webmasters who try to bend and break the rules in their favor by instituting these so-called Black-Hat SEO techniques. So the important lesson to learn from all of this is that you need to take a very organic approach to your blogging. What does this mean? It means that you need to really do the work here if you want optimal long-term results. However, it doesn't mean that you can't use what I like to call *Grey Hat SEO* techniques, which tend to straddle the fence between the Black-Hats and the White-Hats.

Grey Hat SEO straddles the fence between the Black and the White because in essence you are following the rules that Google has set forth in its Webmaster Guidelines, but you are just leveraging certain services that will make your life easier. Because as you'll come to find in this book, the primary driving factor behind SEO is link authority. Link authority essentially refers to how many Websites link to you and how good those links are. But link authority has recently been beefed up to also include social media shares from the big three, including Google Plus, Facebook, and Twitter. The more Tweets, Plus Ones, and Facebook Likes and Shares you have, the more relevant you are in the eyes of Google.

As you'll come to find, building links back to your Website is going to be one of the most arduous tasks that you'll be engaging in as a blogger, especially when you're first starting out. As your blog grows, and your readership expands to a large group of regulars, link building will get easier because those regulars will begin sharing your content on their own. However, in the beginning you need a little bit of a kick to get things started.

In the pages of this book I will be outlining what I consider Grey Hat SEO techniques, along with their White-Hat SEO counterparts. You can decide on your own based on the information provided which direction you choose to travel in. However, my goal really for you in this book is to help you build a solid foundational understanding for how to rank your blog on Google as fast as possible without getting Sandboxed. Yes, Sandboxed. Google has a virtual Sandbox that it throws Websites into that misbehave and the Sandbox is a product of the new search environment since the algorithm updates.

Sound overwhelming? Well, it may seem that way right now, but as you read through the pages of this book you will begin to gain a thorough understanding of just how the SEO industry works. Because without this information, you could potentially harm your site by engaging in practices that may at first seem relatively harmless, when in fact they can completely destroy your capability to rank high on Google's SERPs.

THE GOOGLE SANDBOX

As a result of all the algorithm changes that were instituted by Google, it came up with a virtual sandbox where it would place Websites that either misbehaved, or were new to the playing field. The *Google Sandbox Effect* is a well-documented effect that reaches across the Web and penalizes Websites for either being too new or instituting what it considers Black-Hat SEO techniques to push its way up Google's SERPs.

The one thing that you don't want to have happen is to end up in Google's Sandbox, because your blog could sit and languish on the Web for a long time before you begin getting some serious traffic. This is due to the fact that your blog's articles won't start appearing at the top of Google's SERPs, even if they are perfectly written and perfectly optimized. This will happen when you either never earned Google's trust in the first place, or you instituted some practices that broke Google's trust and it penalized you for it.

This is why with a new or existing blog, you must tread carefully. If you try to force your rankings too hard, Google will penalize you for it. That's because Google stores the amount of links that are generated each day to every site along with a plethora of other information about those links. Although it doesn't release its numbers of what number of links constitutes being involved in "link schemes," if Google sees that you have only a handful of links to your site one month, then the next month you have thousands of links, it's certainly going to raise some red flags. This will get Google to begin not to trust you.

In Google's Webmaster Guidelines, it outlines what it considers its quality guidelines for any Website on the Web. They state that these "quality guidelines cover the most common forms of deceptive or manipulative behavior, but Google may respond negatively to other misleading practices not listed here. It's not safe to assume that just because a specific deceptive technique isn't included on this page, Google approves of it." For this reason, you must tread very carefully, especially if you are new to the SEO scene and you don't have a lot of experience behind your belt.

In general, in order not to end up in Google's Sandbox, you should make sure that you adhere to the following practices on your blog:

- Don't try to write your blog articles and Webpage content only for Google's search engine. Even if you are writing your content from an SEO perspective, you need to make sure that the article sounds as natural as possible. Don't try to stuff keywords into the article just to hit a certain keyword density (I will discuss keyword density in the coming chapters), or make the article sound unnatural or spammy in any way.

- Don't try to deceive your blog's visitors. Whether you're new to blogging and SEO or you're a seasoned veteran, don't try to create content that will trick the users into thinking that your page is about something that it's not about just to optimize for a certain keyword. If you're blogging about a specific keyword or topic, stay on that topic, and don't try to stuff other information in there.

- Always provide value on your Website. If your Website is unique and engaging and provides excellent content, Google will pick up on this based on what's called the stickiness factor. If you have Google Analytics installed, Google will actually take into account just how much time people spend on your site's pages and adjust your rankings for those blog articles accordingly. Always write excellent articles. Always.

- Don't try to trick the Google search engine. These are Black-Hat SEO techniques that you should never institute on your blog. If you put these into play, you could risk more than low rankings. You could be risking a full de-indexing off of Google's search results entirely. Here are the specific techniques that you should not be using on your blog:

○ **Sneaky redirects** – Whether you're savvy enough to do redirects using PHP or other Web programming code, you shouldn't do this. Don't ever try to trick the Website visitor by pushing them to a different page, no matter what the reason you may have.

○ **Content cloaking** – This happens when Webmasters try to conceal the real content of their page to the search engines. They make an entirely different page appear to the search engines than to human eyes. Don't ever try to do this, or risk severe penalties from Google.

○ **Automatically generating content** – Don't try to automatically generate content for your blog article by using Web-based programming languages. Make sure that the content is static and very laser focused on your tags and keywords.

○ **Scraping content from the Web** – Never duplicate content from another Website, just to add volume to your own. This is very bad and will result in severe penalties from Google for your overall site's articles and pages. Always set out to write unique, well-researched content that's never duplicated.

o **Adding irrelevant keywords to your pages** – Don't try to stuff in keywords that don't pertain to the blog article's content. This also includes not adding tags to your articles that don't apply. Be very specific and hone your keywords and tags for your articles.

o **Hiding text or links using font colors and CSS** – Another very bad practice that used to be instituted by a lot of Webmasters. Don't try to hide text and links by masking it with font colors at the bottom of the page, or hidden in CSS layers. Google will severely penalize you for this these days.

o **Creating doorway pages** – these are low quality pages written specifically to rank for a certain keyword. This also includes not creating pages specially designed to generate traffic for affiliate programs without having high-quality content on the page.

o **Creating pages with malicious behavior** – Never ever create pages that inject ads, pop-ups, install viruses, Trojans, and so on. This may go without saying to some, but others still try to use deceptive practices to lure in users. Never do this or risk severe penalties from Google.

THE APPROACH

A blog article is judged in accordance to three major components for ranking. These are the components that Google utilizes to determine just how high, or low, it's going to rank that particular listing. Once you come to understand the bigger picture of how Google's algorithm functions, you'll have a better idea of what changes you can institute that will help your own particular situation site-wide, as well as how to best craft your blog articles so that those specific listings rank high.

The three major components involved with ranking of a blog for SEO are all based upon trust and relevancy and how much Google trusts your site and thinks your blog posts are relevant. Google will determine trust through the age of the domain and backlinking, and it will determine relevancy through content. I will go into details on these three components to better help you understand just how Google is going to judge your site and your article posts in general. But overall, Google will take these three components and compute a relevancy ranking, therefor slipping you into one of its search listing positions based upon this.

The whole point of a Google search is this relevancy ranking that it obtains by bringing all of this information together. Google wants to display the most relevant search results first, plain and simple. It's been this quest for relevancy that has been the major driving force in each and every algorithm change that was instituted by Google. That's because the Web was heading towards irrelevancy to some degree because Websites were cheating their way to the top of Google's SERPs. What does all this mean? Well, you have to ensure that when you're blogging, that you're blogging the right way.

What is blogging the right way?

When I talk about blogging the right way, I'm referring to providing high-quality content that is tailored for Google SEO. Because when all these changes were made to Google's algorithm, they really started targeting low-quality content that was trying to cheat its way to the top. Your quality has to be high quality and it has to be well researched. Take the time to actually research the subject that you're writing about, and provide an in-depth article that solves a problem for your blog readers.

Think about it. When you do searches on Google, and you're looking for some particular information, the Website that you usually end up finding that information on is a blog. It can be any variety of blog types, but usually the information resides on a blog that provides primarily that type of content. The article fits the blog niche. That's because blogs that have all of their articles in one particular niche, usually rank higher. When Google sees articles all in a similar niche from the same domain name that are all well written and optimized for SEO, the overall ranking of the site improves on the whole.

Of course, most bloggers will blog in one particular niche, but some blogs will be very diverse, which actually dulls the chances of higher rankings on the whole. This isn't to say that if you blog about fashion, you can't have a blog post about politics or electronics from time to time, but it won't rank as high. That's because the tags associated with your blog will primarily be in the fashion industry so your blog will begin increasing in presence for fashion. When you throw an entirely different blog article in there from an entirely different industry, it won't rank as high.

By ensuring that your blog is well written, well researched, unique, provides value, and is written from an SEO perspective, you will begin to earn Google's trust. When you begin earning Google's trust, your articles will start to appear at the top of its search results more regularly. However, earning Google's trust takes time, which is why you hear about bloggers being successful only after many years of blogging. That's because they earned Google's trust over time, and as the years wore on, their blog articles began ranking higher and higher. But this isn't easy to do and it takes a sincere and focused commitment on your part.

EARNING GOOGLE'S TRUST

Let's face it blogging isn't easy. To be a great blogger not only do you have to write really good articles, but you also have to write really good articles that are tailored to a specific keyword. When you can master the art of this, and you have the other components in place, then you will begin to see some excellent results from your work. But first you must have all the components in place and ensure that the underlying foundational components of your blog are strong, and if they're not, you need to make it that way. Google is going to base its trust and relevancy ranking on these three factors.

1. Trust through age

2. Trust through authority

3. Trust through content

Trust through Age

Google trusts Websites that it's known about for two or more years. In order to be able to unlock your true ranking potential, it has to have indexed your Website at least two or more years ago. This new ranking algorithm has only come about in the past few years and it is a product of the Google Panda & Penguin updates. Google no longer allows new Websites and blogs to skyrocket to the top of its search results unless it's been around for a while.

This is what you would call having an aged domain name. You're going to have difficulties ranking a brand new blog high on Google's search results unless you purchase an aged domain. If you already have your blog this might not really be an option for you, especially if you've invested a good amount of time already in backlinking to your articles, designing a logo, and so on. But, if you haven't started a blog yet, this is your opportunity to gain a small competitive advantage.

What most people don't realize out there is that you can actually purchase aged domains. You gain a competitive advantage by doing this because Google now recognizes you as someone it knows. It's similar to walking into a bank and trying to get a business loan. New business loans are very difficult, whereas loans for existing businesses that have a track record are considerably easier. When you have a track record, Google knows that it can trust your article posts so the search engine will be much more likely to rank you higher faster.

However, when you're looking to purchase an aged domain name, you have to ensure that the historical content of the domain name is going to match your own content. If Google sees you trying to take a domain name that it indexed in the past for healthcare related services, and finds you doing a blog about finance and money, you may end up getting penalized for it. In order to avoid this, make sure that when you're looking to purchase an aged domain name, that you do so with congruency to your intended future content. I'll be discussing this in more detail in the coming chapters.

Trust through Authority

Authority is what's created when other important Websites link to your blog. In order to build authority, you have to do so over time, which is another reason why aged domain names are great because they have built authority over time already (in most cases). Remember, it's an aged domain name based on the first time Google indexed the domain and not the first date it was registered. But building trust through authority is probably one of the most difficult parts of blogging because it takes a lot of real work.

A few years ago, before Google instituted its algorithm changes, you could build trust through authority very easily. You could in effect cheat Google. You could cheat Google by running what they now consider link-schemes, a Black-Hat SEO technique. However, there are a lot of different kinds of "link schemes," some that are more severe than others. But if you know what you're doing, you could expedite the trust through authority by using what I would consider to be a modified backlinking program. I'll be discussing this in more detail as well.

But to understand trust through authority, you have to understand how Websites on the Internet rank in general. They use something created by Google called PageRank. The PageRank of a Website is essentially indicative of the importance of it. A PageRank of 10 is the most important, which refers to Websites like Google and Facebook, whereas a PageRank of 0 is the least important. A brand new Website with no content, no authority links, and a new domain name would have a PageRank of 0. Your goal for your blog is to get as many high PageRank Websites to link to you as possible in order to increase your own PageRank.

The links to your blog should also be as diverse as possible. They should be coming from different types of Websites around the world. Meaning they should be coming from Websites with different IP addresses, especially when it comes to the lower PageRank Websites. Creating 100 different links on the same Website doesn't have the same effect as doing so on 100 different Websites spread out across the world. This creates what's called IP diversification and tells Google that your site is important because many different and diverse Websites are linking to you. Aside from that, the links should be going to as many different pages of your blog as possible. They shouldn't all be directed to the home page. I will be discussing all of the details of building trust through authority in the coming chapters.

Trust through Content

I'm sure you've heard this before, but content certainly is king. Writing really good content is one of the major hurdles in blogging. As long as you can write really good content that provides value and is unique, you can build trust through authority quickly in the eyes of Google. But this comes back down to the notion that your content should be congruent. If you are a fashion blogger, then do all fashion blog posts and make sure that they all provide value and are well written. One bad apple here can spoil the bunch.

You can build trust through content with Google by not duplicating content. If Google finds that you've duplicated content, your blog will get penalized. This is the biggest no-no in the SEO industry. Never duplicate content. Never. Make sure that you approach each blog post with a mission to write the best possible piece that you can. It's better to do this, than it is to write several subpar blog posts each day. Spend your time on that one really good blog post in the day and make it count.

But building trust through content also comes down to writing your blog articles from an SEO perspective. In the coming chapters I will discuss with you just how to do the keyword research and tailor your articles to best optimize them for Google's search engine to give you the biggest opportunity for visibility that you can possibly get. This will be a major portion of your time spent on doing this, however, there are some invaluable tools that can help speed up this process of optimizing your articles for Google's search engine. But it's best to understand how this works from the beginning so that you can keep it in mind when writing your articles and not have to solely rely on these tools.

2
BUILDING TRUST THROUGH AGE

Building trust through age takes time. Over the years, Google will begin to trust your blog more and more as it finds more well written, unique articles that provide value to the Web. As Google begins to find your articles over time, your trust through age will increase. However, most people just don't want to wait years and years for Google to begin trusting their Website.

If you're stuck with a particular domain name that's virtually brand new, you may want to consider switching your blog to an aged domain. An aged domain is a domain that has been indexed by Google two or more years ago. However, you have to be somewhat careful in the process of purchasing an aged domain. A couple of guidelines:

- **Always purchase an aged domain with content congruency** – You should always look to purchasing an aged domain that has content that will be similar to the type of blog articles you intend to post. Don't try to deviate from this just because you found a really good aged domain name. It's better to have content congruency than a name that sounds really good, so if you have to pick between the two then select the former over the latter.

- **Always purchase an aged domain with the highest historical traffic** – You should always purchase an aged domain name with a good historical traffic track record. You can utilize the Internet's Wayback Machine in order to determine historical track record along with historical content. This one Website tool will help you properly analyze the aged domain name that you intend to purchase.

Now, these are just the guidelines for purchasing an aged domain name, but one thing you have to keep in mind when doing this is that you may always run the risk of purchasing an aged domain name that was Sandboxed in the past. There's no real way of telling what domains were Sandboxed by Google for violating their Webmaster Guidelines, so you have to be careful when doing this and do your research. Although you'll never be able to tell if a domain was Sandboxed, the rewards in purchasing an aged domain name outweigh the risks in doing so.

As I will be discussing in the coming sections, you can use online tools to analyze traffic patterns to see if there were any major dips or drop offs in Traffic for the domain you may consider purchasing, in the past. Although this won't be a direct indicator of Sandboxing (it could mean the domain was transferred, or just taken off line), if you don't see any major drop offs in traffic, it's a good tell tale sign that historically the domain name was okay as far as Sandboxing.

USING GODADDY AUCTIONS

In order to find the aged domains for purchase, you can use a number of online domain auction sites, but the most reliable one that I've found is GoDaddy Auctions. Just navigate your browser to http://auctions.godaddy.com and the process in purchasing an aged domain is somewhat similar to that of purchasing a brand new domain. The major difference you are going to encounter is that the aged domain will take a few days up to about a week to transfer to you after the purchase is complete.

Aged domains are terrific because if you do your due diligence first, then you're really almost buying the shell of an old business. This shell is going to give you a competitive advantage when it comes to SEO, but only if you do the proper due diligence. This is going to give your blog a very good head start because it's going to give you an existing track record that will make Google much more likely to trust you. To get started hunting for an aged domain name, simply click on the advanced search link to the right of the search box on the GoDaddy Auctions homepage.

The reason you want to conduct an advanced search is so that you can input and select certain criteria that you want the domain name to adhere to in your search. This criterion is what will make the domain name the most attractive from an aged domain perspective. The great thing about GoDaddy Auctions is that you'll be able to find domain names that are newly expired and have not been renewed for any number of reasons. These names are ideal and this usually occurs due to the carelessness of the domain name holders. I have been able to locate some pretty incredible domain names through this single resource.

A myth I want to dispel here, however, is that aged domain names are expensive, because they are not. You will pay no more for an aged domain name than you would for a brand new domain name as long as you don't buy it at auction. When you select the "Buy Now Option" in the advanced search you can find domain names that you don't have to bid on and you can purchase immediately. These are the optimal targets for your search. You can usually find domain names through this resource for only a few dollars more than what you would pay had you decided to purchase the domain names brand new anywhere on the Web. This is a terrific way to get a head start on your blog in terms of SEO.

After you click on the "advanced search" link to the right of the search box on the GoDaddy Auctions homepage, you'll need to adjust some of the settings from the default as shown in the proceeding image. Here's what we're looking for:

- **Keywords** – If you want to have a specific keyword in your domain name, then enter that in here but make sure you change the drop-down box to say, "contains" instead of, "exact match." If you leave it as exact match, it will only return results that are exactly that keyword, which is going to be very rare. For example, if you are blogging about Apple products, then you may want to have the keyword "Mac," or "Apple" in the domain name. You can experiment with adding a keyword and leaving it out.

- **Extensions** – Make sure that you check the ".com" checkbox on your first search. If you cannot find a good domain name with a ".com" extension, then you can broaden the search, but you shouldn't have a problem finding one. You can always modify your keywords or leave out the keyword in order to get a broader results set back with ".com" domain names.

- **Attributes** – Under the attributes section, check off the "Buy Now Option" checkbox. This will return domain auctions that are available for immediate purchase and won't involve a lengthy bidding or auction process.

- **Domain Age** – You want to look for domain names that are 5 years old and up. You can settle for one that is 2 or 3 years and up, however, there always seems to be a large supply of domain names that are 5 years and upwards of 15 years aged in the GoDaddy Auctions system. If you leave out the keywords you are most likely to find much older domain names.

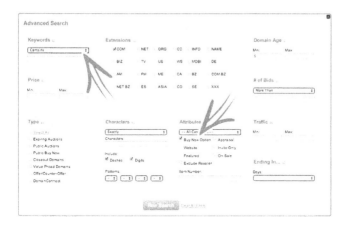

Once you've inputted the criteria for the aged domain name search, you'll be presented with a number of options based on the variables that you provided. Namely, if you used a keyword, you'll see results tailored to that, or none if there are no matching domains available. In the proceeding image, you'll see the results of a search where I used the keyword "travel," set the extension to ".com," selected the "Buy Now Option" checkbox, and placed in a minimum domain age of 5 years.

There were numerous results that came back for that search. When you conduct a search, after it's complete click on the "traffic" tab in order to sort by traffic from ascending to descending. You'll want to go after domain names with the highest traffic results. Once that's complete, and you see the best names as far as traffic from the top down to the bottom, click on the "+ "symbols to expand the details of the domain auction. When you do that, you'll be provided with information such as the price, status, age, and so on.

But your work is not done here. We want to find out the first time these domain names were indexed by Google, and not the first time the domain was registered. The number of years provided by GoDaddy only tells you the number of years ago the name was initially registered by the current registrant. However, that domain name could be considerably older than that number. But the problem with that is that, the domain could have been registered and sat idle for years so it's important to take this a further step to see just when Google found it. The first time the domain was indexed by Google will indicate its true age. To find its true age you have to use the Internet's Wayback Machine. You can find it at the following URL: http://archive.org/web/web.php

As you analyze each of the domain names, type them into the Wayback Machine in order to return the results of the traffic. You should see spikes of traffic over the years that would indicate how much traffic the domain name received. Now this won't tell you whether or not the domain has been Sandboxed in the past, but strong traffic over a consistent historical period of time is a good indication that the domain was not Sandboxed, but it's not a guarantee. If you see traffic drop off significantly, that could be an indication of Sandboxing if it happened sometime after 2011. However, it could also just mean that the domain was transferred, or the registrant took the Website offline or the company went out of business.

Take a look at the age indicated by GoDaddy Auctions to see whether or not that during the age represented by GoDaddy, there were any major pitfalls in traffic. Look closely at the period from 2011 to the present day. For example, if a domain name age is 6 years old as indicated by GoDaddy Auctions, and you see a major drop in traffic sometime in mid-2011 or any other period around or after that time, it could mean the domain was Sandboxed by Google. It could have been a victim of the Google Panda or the Google Penguin.

In the proceeding image, you'll see the traffic analysis for Yahoo.com. As you would expect, the traffic is very strong historically with a gradual increase over time. Obviously we all know that Yahoo has strong historical traffic, but the great thing about this online tool is you can use it to analyze any Website's history. In addition, you can actually see archived screenshots of the Website over time. This is an excellent way you can help to ensure that the historical congruency between the domain name and your intended use for your blog exists. This is probably one of the most important parts of engaging in this process. Look at the specific pages in the Wayback Machine's archives to see what type of pages they were and if they would align with your blog's intended future content.

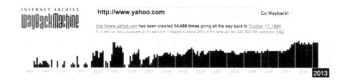

Use the tool to check the history of the domain names that you find in search results and select a domain name based on what you find. Use your best judgment, but don't be afraid to spend some time on this search. You may want to come back every couple of days to see what's available because really good domain names go up for auction each and every single day, so depending on how lucky you are you may end up getting an excellent domain name at a very reduced cost. Also, if you're a budget shopper, you can find GoDaddy Discount Codes on the following Website: http://www.retailmenot.com but they may or may not have discount codes available for auctions so you have to just check and try different codes that may be available at the time you're reading this.

After you've purchased your domain name, keep in mind that the transfer will take a few days to up to a week. You will get an email from GoDaddy when your domain name's transfer has been complete. However, to see the current status of your purchase transfer, click on "Bidding List," as shown in the proceeding image, and in the drop-down menu click on the "Won" tab. This will show you the auctions that you have won and the dates the transfers will be complete. When the transfer is complete you will receive a final email from GoDaddy with the information. You can then use that domain name to setup a hosted Wordpress configuration with any hosting provider you choose.

Purchasing an aged domain name is what I would consider to be a *Grey-Hat SEO* technique. This is not frowned upon and people have been doing this for quite some time, but it's something that is little known to the average bloggers or search engine marketers on the Web. Again, you have to tread with caution here and don't purchase a domain name that has entirely different historically indexed content than your future intended purchases for it. If you stay congruent to historical content, you shouldn't have problems down the line, but again there's no guarantee that the domain was never

Sandboxed. Still, in my opinion, the rewards of owning an aged domain name far outweigh its risks.

3
BUILDING A FRAMEWORK FOR SEO

Content is king. It's plain and simple. The better your blog articles are, the more likely you are to appear at the top of Google's search results as long as you properly satisfied the other components of trust: age and authority. We'll get to authority in the next few chapters. However, for the time being, it's important that you build a framework for your content that will allow Google to trust your blog. In another words, the layout and design of your blog is critical to the overall success of your SEO efforts.

Without the proper framework for your content, you won't have the ability to potentially rank as high as possible. And since the name of the game is rankings here, you want to ensure that you're as compliant as possible with Google's set of rules for your Website. In essence, Google is looking for a few things here, but really it all boils down to user experience. User experience was the big factor for their first major algorithm change, the Google Panda. Since the Penguin is the evolution of the Panda, user experience is still critical but is more likely now rolled into its base-ranking algorithm.

Back in January of 2012, Google actually identified this algorithm update on their Google Webmaster Central Blog where they stated that based upon their research, users were frustrated with Websites when they couldn't get to the content immediately. "Rather than scrolling down the page past a slew of ads, users want to see content right away." For this reason, users don't want to have to scroll past a lot of different ads and other distractors to find the content. They want to find the content close to the top.

If you're unfamiliar with the Website's fold, that's the part of your blog that gets cut off after the page loads and a scroll bar is required to access the balance of the Webpage. The content that doesn't get cut off is considered content that is above the fold. The content that does get cut off and requires scrolling to access, is considered content that is below the fold. You have to ensure that your blog's graphics and header do not take up too much space above the fold of the Website.

Most people may wonder what the exact dimensions in pixels are for the Website's fold, but there are no specific pixels defined. Instead, you must guestimate based on average screen resolutions, and depending on when you're reading this that will most likely vary. Use your best judgment here but if you're up in the air about whether or not your header graphics consume too much of the Website's fold then it probably does. Remember to keep it as simple as possible. You don't want people scouring for the content, or bombarded with text and background colors that make them want to scream and run for the door.

Overall, there are a few other guidelines that you need to ensure that your blog adheres to. You'll want to either follow these guidelines as you configure your blog, or go back into your configuration and ensure that you blog is meeting the specifications laid out in the following list.

- **Give your blog a clear hierarchy and text links** – Every single page of your blog should be reachable from at least one static text link. When you setup your blog, depending on the theme you choose (whether it's a custom theme or a standard theme) you have to make sure that the hierarchy is clear. This comes back to the user experience because if a user is confused and has difficulty navigating your site, then so will the Google search engine spiders, and your site will be penalized as a result.

- **Make sure that there are no broken links** – This may go without saying to you, but Google cares more about this now than ever before. When there are broken links on a blog or Website, users get frustrated. Users get frustrated because broken links make a site hard to navigate. Since Google is focused on providing top search listings that give users an excellent user experience, you won't rank high if your site is riddled with broken links.

- **Create an XML sitemap** – A sitemap is critical, and without one, your blog won't be fully optimized for Google. I know, creating a sitemap seems so superfluous, but it's actually something that Google requires in their design and content guidelines for Webmasters. When using Wordpress, an excellent free Google sitemap generator plugin can be found at the following URL: http://bit.ly/xmlsitemapplugin

- **Use text instead of images** – The Web used to be wrought with images used for everything from navigational elements to titles, and overall images used to be littered throughout Websites. Those days have gone because today you can achieve just about any image effect with CSS. Ensure that you use text anytime it's possible because Google simply cannot read images. Use text for links always and everywhere else possible. Try not to ever place text into image files if it can be avoided.

- **Utilize robots.txt** – This file will control the behavior of search engine spiders such as Google when they arrive at your blog. By inserting certain text, you can modify the behavior of the search engines. For example, you should block Google from crawling any administration files like the Wordpress admin, and any dynamic files, search results or directories on your site. Here is an example of a robots.txt file that you can use for your Wordpress blog. You'll need to place the robots.txt file in the root directory of your blog or Website. The sitemap line in the proceeding image must be replaced with your own domain and filename.

```
User-agent: *
Disallow: /feed/
Disallow: /trackback/
Disallow: /wp-admin/
Disallow: /wp-content/
Disallow: /wp-includes/
Disallow: /xmlrpc.php
Disallow: /wp-
Allow: /wp-content/uploads/
Sitemap: http://example.com/sitemap.xml
```

- **Cross-browser compatibility** – Make sure that your blog appears the same across multiple browsers such as Internet Explorer, Firefox, Chrome and Safari. Also make sure that the site loads quickly and is not bogged down by overly excessive video or graphic-heavy imagery. This all adds into the user experience, and by ensuring for an optimal user experience, your blog has a better chance of ranking high on Google's SERPs.

Some of these bullet points may sound somewhat obvious to you and some may not. The problem with hiring a Web designer oftentimes is that they usually don't assist in making sure that a Website is completely SEO compliant so you have to be vigilant on your own. If you've hired someone to customize your blog or Website, ask a lot of questions and ensure things like the robots.txt file has been placed in the root, and that the important text is above the fold.

Overall keep the framework of your Website simple. Don't make too much going on in the form of graphics and ads before users can get to your content. Just imagine yourself surfing the Web, looking for information. When the eye gets scattered across the screen and the page looks busy, most of us tend to click away. Your traffic is a precious commodity and you should do whatever it takes within your power to preserve your Website's stickiness (time spent on the blog by visitors).

GOOGLE WEBMASTER TOOLS

One of the most invaluable tools you can utilize when you're your own SEO conductor is the Google Webmaster Tools. This suite of tools will provide you with some powerful insight into your Website and it will also allow you to inform Google of your site and submit your XML sitemaps as well. You may receive notifications from Google through the Webmaster tools from time to time informing you if anything is amiss with your blog or site. If Google can't access your pages for some reason, it can't crawl your robots.txt file, and so on, it will notify you automatically.

To access Google Webmaster Tools and to add your Website in, you'll need a Google account first. If you don't have one, you can set one up at the following URL that will give you access to the Webmaster Tools: http://www.google.com/webmasters/tools. After setting up your Google Webmaster Tools account, be sure to add your Website and your sitemap URL. Use the sitemap generator free plugin for Wordpress in order to generate a sitemap - http://bit.ly/xmlsitemapplugin.

The Google Webmaster Tools will also provide you with invaluable information that Google uses in ranking Websites. Since you already know that your Website's load time, link errors, and other factors affects your ranking, you can utilize the Webmaster Tools to help you debug any errors you may have going forward. The Webmaster tools provides you with powerful insights that include:

- The ability to submit and check your sitemap file.

- Provide Google with a crawl rate for accessing your site on a periodic basis should you choose to have it do so.

- Generate a robots.txt file, and discover files that may be blocked by robots.txt.

- Find links (both external and internal) to your Website.

- Find broken links.

- See the different keyword searches that are being used to access your Website and what the click-through rates of those keywords are.

- View and analyze statistics on how Google indexes your blog and if it found any errors while doing so.

Since you'll be conducting your own SEO work, that work is going to involve the analysis of your efforts. Google Webmaster Tools provides you with a great resource to see the amount of impressions that your keywords are making, compared to the amount of clicks you're receiving. It will also provide you with breakdowns that include the average position per keyword on Google's SERPs. Without this knowledge it would be difficult to track the potentially hundreds of keywords associated to your blog's various articles.

GOOGLE ANALYTICS

Google's own analytics engine is another powerful resource for analyzing your blog's traffic and this is something that will play an integral role in your SEO work. Google Analytics has changed so much over the years. Of course, like other Google services, it was purchased from another company and integrated into their own suite of Google product, but Google Analytics is vital. It's vital because it allows you to gain insight that you wouldn't normally be able to find on your own. It shows you patterns of traffic analysis, where those visitors are coming from, what pages they are accessing, demographic info, time spent on pages, and so on.

The newest version of Google Analytics includes asynchronous code, which allows the system to track even very short Website visits. In the past, this wasn't really possible and very short visits to sites didn't get logged. The system is free to use, but there is also a premium version available for a fee. To setup a Google Analytics account, go to: http://www.google.com/analytics. You can easily integrate your Google Analytics account into your Wordpress blog. There are several free plugins available to do this such as this one - http://bit.ly/analyticspluginwp.

Whereas the Google Webmaster Tools show you overall technical data that includes keyword impressions, click-through rates, and other potential site error messages, the analytics provides more marketing-related information. When you begin to utilize the Google Analytics system you'll come to understand just how invaluable this resource truly is. You will be able to analyze the overall behavior of visitors to your site and see just how much time people are spending on the various pages, and which pages they are visiting. This will help you determine whether or not your blog articles are interesting and engaging enough. Because remember, that's one of the main goals that Google has as they want to provide value to the users in the form of really good information. The interesting and engaging sites that adhere to all the other rules for usability and content will be ranked higher. If your information is not good, you will probably see high bounce rates from your blog (visitors leaving very shortly after they've arrived).

4
BUILDING TRUST THROUGH CONTENT

Building trust through content by writing relevant well-written blog articles is probably one of the aspects of your SEO work that you will have the most control over. That's because you control the content that you release out there into the blogosphere. And in the world of SEO, content is king and it reigns supreme so it's your duty to create content that creates value, is informative and engaging. Not only is this imperative from a value perspective, because by doing this you will attract more readers and help to spread word of mouth about your blog, but also, Google specifically wants you to do this and since its one of the major components involved in ranking your site on its SERPs.

Trust through content comes through what's called On-Page SEO, also sometimes referred to as On-Site SEO. Both terms refer to SEO work that's done on the Website or blog itself, as opposed to away from it. Off-Site

SEO or Off-Page SEO is all work done to optimize a site away from the actual Website itself. That would include things like link building, content marketing through authority sites, and social media sharing. But the On-Page SEO is the easier part because you have total control of it. You get to modify your own blog's content and articles and optimize it to your heart's content. As you do that optimization, you'll have to abide by some guidelines in order to make Google trust that your content is very relevant for any given keyword search.

This building of trust through content really starts at the keyword research phase. You have to find the right keywords that people will be searching for, for each of your articles that you write. Remember, as outlined before, Google doesn't want to see irrelevant keywords, or keywords that don't match the content, so you have to be very specific here. You have to tailor and optimize your content for that given keyword, but you can't over optimize it. That's another pitfall of the aftermath from the algorithm changes. Google has become highly sensitive to sites that try to over optimize their content. If you do this you may end up hurting your site more than helping it so you'll have to engage in a bit of a balancing act.

You have to get really good at creating your content and writing your blogs from an SEO perspective. Because as soon as you master this, your life will become much more easier but it's most likely going to take you a bit of trial and error to get it done. Even when you have all of the information in front of you, there's nothing like some real world experience and trying out different things. The problem is that, since Google never reveals their exact algorithm, it's hard to say what will work exactly aside from having a set of guidelines. Google does everything possible to shroud its algorithm in as much secrecy as possible because it knows that if people know exactly what it is, they will do everything possible to try and get to the top and that defeats the whole purpose of "organic search" to them.

In the beginning, when you get your domain up and running and you start blogging, what I've come to notice in this post Google Panda & Penguin world is that you have to start out slow. By slow I'm more referring to aggressive SEO tactics. If you force it too hard in the beginning, Google will know that you're trying to cheat your way up to the top and it will penalize you for it. And you certainly don't want to end up in the Google Sandbox so you have to tread with caution. Also, don't try to over optimize your articles and make them perfectly optimized for a certain keyword. When you write your content, write freely but pay attention to the primary keyword that you've selected for that specific article.

TOOLS FOR ON-PAGE SEO

In the next chapters I outline the specific instructions for building your content from an SEO perspective in order to generate trust through content. And one of the best Wordpress plugins that I have come across for assisting in that SEO-targeted content tailoring is called SEOPressor. SEOPressor is a Wordpress plugin that has been around for quite some time and it's in its fifth version of release. For newbies, this is the single best possible tool you can use to assist while you craft your content for your Wordpress blog. And it provides some great new asynchronous features in the latest version that allow you to check your content while you write it rather than after you save it or publish it.

Although this isn't a free plugin, the SEOPressor plugin does takes a lot of the guesswork out of refining and optimizing your content while providing you with a running score of how well your content is optimized. It does an excellent job of tabulating the various different elements involved with completely optimizing your content for a specific keyword and provides you with a determination of how well it's scoring. The score is based out of 100%, but it also can go over 100%. Contrary to what you may think, over 100% is not a good thing. This would be considered over optimizing, and it's terrific that the plugin takes over optimization into account.

Another great feature of the SEOPressor plugin is the capability for it to utilize what's called LSI, or latent semantic indexing. Although it uses Microsoft's Bing LSI engine for analysis, it's one of the only plugins on the market that takes LSI into account for Wordpress SEO. LSI is a technology that Google utilizes for ranking Websites, and it relies on variations of words or groups of words for those similar ones that would naturally appear in the language. It uses some complex mathematical computations to come up with the variations that we would normally speak naturally in the course of describing something when not focused on forcibly optimizing for a keyword.

If you were to conduct any keyword search on the Web, you may notice that the first few listings don't match that keyword exactly. That's because those listings are utilizing LSI for ranking, along with other factors. Of course domain age, authority and overall content come into play, but the LSI here provides for the x-factor. By utilizing LSI, Google also is sending a message to the over-optimizers. It knows that SEO Webmasters are trying eagerly to optimize for a specific keyword in the exact particular wording so LSI helps to level that playing field.

I would highly recommend installing and utilizing the SEOPressor system. You can find SEOPressor available for download at the following URL: http://bit.ly/seopressorversion5. Please note, this plugin is not free but it is well worth the small amount of money that you pay to utilize the unique feature set that will allow you determine your relevancy ranking for each blog article or page as you prepare it. This is money well spent.

5
CRAFTING SEO CONTENT

The name of the game is content here, and content certainly is king on the Web, especially in the eyes of Google. The search giant cares about your content on multiple different levels. It cares whether or not that content is unique, first and foremost. If it's not unique, you can throw any chance of ranking high out the window. The worst possible thing you can do when blogging is to copy content. It's been rumored in the past that Google only keeps track of the first and last paragraph of content when checking for duplicate data, but I don't believe this is true. I think that Google keeps track of all Webpage data in its massive global server farms. Regardless, you shouldn't take your chances. Always create unique content. Always.

Google also cares about how much value your content provides. When you're blogging, you have to provide value while being interesting and engaging. Google can determine all of these factors based upon the tools it has at its disposal. It can determine interesting and engaging by using the stickiness factor from Google Analytics, or by comparing it to other documents that have been rated high by users on the Web. Also, considering that most Websites across the globe have Google Analytics installed, Google can utilize that data when building out its ranking algorithms. As for the value portion of how well your content is written, Google has crafted algorithms that can analyze your content to see just how well it is written. It uses mathematical comparisons and algorithms to determine this based upon vocabulary usage, word orientations, grammar, spelling, and various other factors. It knows if your content is good so you have to spend the time writing really good blog articles and Webpage content. Don't try to take any shortcuts here, especially if you're committed to ranking high on Google's SERPs.

When you set about to write your content it has to provide value, be interesting and be engaging, but it also has to be keyword-driven. Google is really looking for a piece of content such as a Webpage, a blog article, or anything else, to have a specific purpose. It wants to be able to identify that purpose quickly and easily, and since Google doesn't look at content with human eyes, it uses its Google Bots and Google Spiders to analyze the data based on some key elements. Here are the elements Google utilizes to analyze the blog article's content:

- **Article length** – Google is looking for a minimum of 500 words here, but longer articles tend to rank better. Try to reach 1000 words without making it sound forced. Natural, well researched, and well-written content that's interesting and engaging here is the key.

- **Article content** – Do not sound spammy, and don't try to force the insertion of keywords within the article's content merely to try to achieve a certain keyword density. Use headings to properly section off the content because one long piece of content will be too confusing to read through. Use sections and images to make the content more user-friendly. Just imagine reading a high-quality article on a blog like Mashable, or on a news-related Website like CNN. Sections and images used to cordon off the large amounts of content in the blogs' articles. This adds to an increase in user experience, and in turn, your ability to rank higher.

- **Keyword density** – Your primary keyword, or the LSI-combined version of it should aim to achieve 2% to 5% density of appearance within the content of the page or article. This means that for every 500 words you should have the primary keyword (and/or the LSI version) appear at least a combined 10 times to as many as a combined 25 times. Going well over 5% keyword density will be considered spammy and will appear forced. Remember, if it doesn't sound natural, don't force it. Write your blog article with keyword density in mind, but in the most natural way you possibly can.

- **Keyword positioning** – Your primary keyword should appear in the first sentence and in the last sentence of your content. Some people think that this should be the first paragraph and last paragraph, but the matter is up for debate. If you can start you content with your keyword, even better, but don't force it. If it doesn't sound natural just make sure it's placed within at least the first and last paragraphs but ideally in the first and last sentences.

- **Outbound links** – It's natural that you would want to link to other Webpages, especially when providing a very informative article on a blog. However, you must add a link attribute that essentially tells Google and other search engines not to follow that link away from your site. The problem is that Wordpress doesn't provide any easy way to do this so you have to enter the HTML editor to edit your links after you create them. When a search engine spider like Google finds links it navigates away from the page, thus decreasing the page's optimization. When you create links add the rel="nofollow" attribute to them. This essentially stops the SEO juice at your page and doesn't allow it to leave. Think of it almost like a dead-end street where SEO can accumulate in your favor. Here's what a link would look like with this attribute:

<a href="http://www.somedomain.com" rel="nofollow">Link to Some Domain on the Web here</a>

- **Internal links** – You should have at least one link to another page within the Webpage of your site's content or blog article. This is considered an internal link. Internal links make the site and the article much easier to navigate, and Google likes to be able to reach different pieces of content on a

Website from within other content on the same site. If you have the capability to turn on breadcrumbs in your Wordpress theme, then ensure that you do so. Breadcrumbs allow easy navigation to search engine spiders like Google.

- **Stylized tags** – A stylized tag is when you change the font style to be either bold, underlined or italicized. A good rule of thumb here is to ensure that you have your primary keyword, or an LSI variation of it, at least once in bold, once in italics and once in underlined font per page or article. This helps to further indicate to Google that the primary objective of the page is this primary keyword.

- **Heading tags** – The heading tags (or subheadings as they are sometimes referred to as) are the H1, H2, and H3 tags that modify the appearance of text on your Website or blog article. You've probably had some experience with changing your text to appear within these tags, however they serve a highly functional purpose rather than just an aesthetic one. Google looks for these tags to further clarify what the Webpage or blog article is about. It also helps to section off the page for a more user-friendly browsing experience. Usually in Wordpress the H1 is already defined for you and its done through the title of the article or page itself, but also appears in the HTML title tag as well. However, you must also utilize the H2 and H3 tags. Use your keyword or an LSI version of it within these other tags once. Don't over do it. If you installed

SEOPressor, it will indicate over usage in subheadings for you with simple little warnings.

- **Image ALT information** - The image ALT tag is the alternative tag that's added to an image in order to indicate to Google what it is. Remember, Google can't read images or text in images so you have to tell Google what the image is. To optimize your blog article or Webpage add your primary keyword, or an LSI variation of it for the ALT tag. You can add the alternative tag directly through the Wordpress interface when you add an image to your article or page through the Wordpress administration.

- **Page title** – The page title must include the primary keyword in it or an LSI variation of it. Your page title is usually defined by the article title or Webpage title in Wordpress, and this is also the 70-character maximum title that appears on Google searches. The page title is also equivalent to the H1 and if you've had any customization done to your Wordpress installation or you plan to, you have to ensure that the H1 tag appears above the fold on the Website. This also usually defines the title of the page located within the <title> tag in the header of the Webpage.

- **Meta description** – The meta description is the 140 character maximum description that shows up in Google searches beneath the title. If the meta description is not defined, Google usually selects a description based on the text of the page on its own. However, Wordpress does not adjust the meta description for each particular article that is posted, which is why the SEOPressor plugin is necessary in order to customize the meta description for each article and page on its own. You can download the SEOPressor Wordpress plugin here - http://bit.ly/seopressorversion5

As you'll notice in the proceeding image, I've given the information provided here in a graphical format as a referral tool that you can continuously check back to as a reference. However, I would highly recommend installing the SEOPressor Wordpress plugin for a couple of reasons. First of all, having an accurate assessment of your On-Page SEO score is invaluable while you teach yourself SEO. Secondly, you won't be able to change the article's meta description without it because the default Wordpress installation doesn't provide for this functionality.

On-Page Optimization

1 Use the primary keyword once in page title <H1> tag, once in an <H2> tag and once in an <H3> tag

2 Use the primary keyword in the first paragraph and in the last paragraph

<H1> How to Stop Smoking Fast </H1>

3 Use the primary keyword in the image ALT tag for the Webpage

4 Use the primary keyword **once in bold font**, *once in italics font*, and once in underlined font

5 Use a primary keyword density of 2% to 5% that sounds natural and flows organically

6 Use the primary keyword in the Webpage or article's meta description

7 Make sure primary keyword shows up in the page title, if you are using Wordpress, turn on permalinks and use the "postname" option

Again, this is where I must stress caution against over optimization. In an effort to be very enthusiastic about your SEO efforts, you may end up over optimizing your pages. The preceding graphic and guidelines are simply an outline that you should follow. However, don't overdo it and force your keyword placement. Yes, you should have the primary keyword appear throughout the content of the page and the stylized sections, but do not try to force it throughout the content. If your content begins sounding "spammy," then it is. Even if it's questionable, rework it and make it sound natural. Natural is the absolute key here when it comes to content. This is where LSI comes into play, and you should try variations of your keyword using LSI.

USING LSI IN YOUR CONTENT

Latent Semantic Indexing, or LSI, is a technology being implemented by Google that has its roots in complex mathematical formulas. LSI is also an application of correspondence analysis first developed in the 1970s by Jean-Paul Benzécri. The term Latent Semantic Indexing stems from the fact that the technology is able to semantically correlate related terms in a latent collection of text. Although it may sound extremely confusing, LSI is in fact a blessing for keyword optimization.

LSI is a terrific way to optimize Webpages in a way that will not only allow you to not have them become considered as spammy, but also allows you to write text more freely. For example, if you were to take the keyword "how to lose weight fast," there are only so many times you can use the keyword in that exact same grouping of words without having the text sound unnatural and spammy within say a 1000 word article. This is where LSI comes into play. Here are some variations of that keyword using LSI:

- Quick weight loss methods

- Ways to lose weight fast

- How to quickly lose weight

- Fast Weight loss tips

Can you see the correlation now between the keywords? Now, you might be asking yourself the question, "Well, if I use an LSI variation of my keyword, what keyword density should I use?" When you optimize your article or Webpage for the keyword "how to lose weight fast," for example, you should stick to placing the keyword as is in a 3 to 5 ratio. That is for every 3 times you use the keyword "how to lose weight fast," you should use its LSI counterparts two times. Since you want to achieve a keyword density of 2% to 5% that means that in a 1000 word article, you would normally have to have a keyword density of 20 to 50 keywords. Now, this would be very difficult to do without using LSI and would run the risk of sounding very spammy. For that reason, you can use the primary keyword exactly as is 12 to 30 times and use its LSI counterparts 8 to 20 times.

6

ON THE HUNT FOR KEYWORDS

Blogging effectively is really all about finding the right keywords, then crafting your article content to fit that keyword. It sounds simple enough, but all too often people forgo the most important parts of ensuring that the articles are well researched and well written. You have to add value or your content is simply not going to rank. I can't stress that point enough. Especially in today's highly competitive search engine landscape, if you're blogging without adding value, then you might as well not blog.

If you've blogged in the past and found it difficult to get ranked on Google's search engine, well, that's because it is difficult. But, if you follow along by building trust through the various components such as age, content and authority, over time your content will rank high on Google's SERPs consistently. But, blogging is a serious commitment and so is SEO, so it's better that you gain a clear understanding of how to blog effectively from the get go. Yes, you must be an excellent writer and be able to engage and add value, but you must also be able to do so in a way that shows Google you're relevant. And that relevancy is gleaned from targeting your articles to your keywords.

It's also important to blog for keywords that you know you'll be able to rank for. Or in another words, keywords that have lower competition. It's very difficult to rank high for keywords that have high competition. Even for blogs that have been around for years and are trusted by Google, since there is so much competition, you really have to go above and beyond with your underlying article content. However, it's far easier to rank high for low-competition keywords. And usually, the low-competition keywords exist in what are called *long-tail keywords*. Long-tail keywords have as few as four words in them, but can generally have upwards of 8 to 10. For example, you will have a much easier time ranking for "how to lose weight in 30 days," than simply "how to lose weight." The longer the keyword, the easier it will be to rank, and this is one of the primary strategies when starting out with your blog.

In the beginning, this should be your primary focus. Concentrate your blog articles on long-tail keywords so that you can gain some rank quickly because it's better to be ranked at the top of a Google search with low volume than nowhere to be found on a search with high volume. As time goes on and your blog builds authority, you will be able to rank high for short-tail keywords as well. It's also going to take you some time practicing your blogging skills on a daily basis. Each day you'll refine your SEO blogging craft better and better until you'll be a pro in no time.

But it all starts out with the keywords and the first thing that you need to learn how to do is keyword research. It's in this keyword research phase that you'll be able to judge some very important factors when it comes to the keywords that you may plan on writing blogs about such as:

- How many people search for the keyword per month globally

- How many people search for the keyword each month locally

- How many other related keyword searches there are

- How much competition there is for the keyword

Based upon this very helpful information that you'll receive after conducting your keyword research, you'll be able to focus in on the keywords that make the most sense to target. And of course, the best keywords are those that have little competition and high search volume, but they may be few and far between. You will be much more likely to find that the long-tail keywords fit this description than the short-tail keywords.

HOW TO FIND KEYWORDS

Finding the right keywords takes some good hearty research. As you sit down to brainstorm your blog posts, you'll find yourself including keyword research in your daily activities. That's because, it only really makes sense to blog for a specific keyword. You don't want to blog about something out of the blue, even though you may be inclined to do so. These types of blogs confuse Google, and instead, your blog posts should be laser-focused around a target keyword.

By utilizing some simple online tools, you can effectively research the keyword that you're interested in blogging about by using an online resource provided by Google called the Google Adwords Keyword Tool. No, this doesn't mean that you need to run ads on Google. However, this is the same tool used by the search giant to provide relevant data to its advertisers looking to sell ads on its sites. You know, the ads that appear to the right of the SERP listings, in YouTube videos, in Gmail emails, and so on.

The great thing is that you can leverage this existing tool, which provides all the data that you'll need in your hunt for keywords, for your own blog posts. The Google Adwords Keyword Tool provides you with the information to form an educated opinion on whether or not you'll be able to rank for a certain keyword. It will give you the supply and demand of that keywords search results. Because by knowing the supply and demand of the SERP listings, you'll be able to accurately gauge how well you can potentially rank.

This is a practice that you'll get much more accustomed to over time. You'll find yourself doing the keyword research before setting about to do your blog posts, then being able to effectively track those keywords using both the Google Webmaster Tools and Google Analytics. It will be a process that you'll get used to, but first things first: keyword research.

To start out with researching your keywords head over to the Google Adwords Keyword Tool Website. You can either Google the term "keyword tool," and pick the first listing on Google's SERP. Or, you can also simply type in the following URL in your browser to find the tool online: https://adwords.google.com/o/KeywordTool

Aside from using the Google Adwords Keyword Tool, you will also be using a free plugin called SEO Quake. SEO Quake will allow you to see in-depth results on a search to see just what components are making the top listings rank the way they rank. SEO Quake is almost like putting on a pair of x-ray glasses and seeing through Google's SERPs to find what information the search giant is using to tabulate its rankings. It will show you the inner workings of the domain name and the Webpage that the listing resides on. The plugin is available on Firefox and Internet Explorer, and there is an extension available for Google Chrome.

SEO Quake is a free plugin or extension, so depending on which browser you use, you'll need to get SEO Quake installed so that you can use it in the keyword research process. The overall keyword research process for your blog articles will go something like this:

- Brainstorm then search for keywords on Google Adwords Keyword Tool.

- Compare keywords based on their competition and search volumes to select a few keywords that you can then test.

- Use the SEO Quake toolbar to finalize your research by testing the top listings on a keyword SERP to see if you will be able to compete for that search.

One recommendation that I would offer up is that you shouldn't install SEO Quake on the browser that you use on an everyday basis. That's because SEO Quake adds in a small toolbar under each SERP listing that clutters the page when you're not intending on doing keyword research. Install it on a secondary browser that you can use when conducting your keyword research. So if you use Internet Explorer most of the time, then install it on Firefox or Chrome. Also, SEO Quake is not available for Safari as of the present date and there's no indication that it will be.

Installation of SEO Quake is fairly straightforward. You should install the plugin or extension on the browser of your choice. However, SEO Quake does have some settings that you will need to be aware of. These settings control how much data is presented on the toolbar. You can either select to have a lot of data appear, or only a little. But there are some vital pieces of data that you are going to want to know about. Those would include things like:

1. Whois - Shows domain's age

2. SEMRush links – Shows number of links to the page

3. SEMRush linkdomain – Shows number of links to the domain

4. Twitter Tweets

5. Facebook likes

6. Google PlusOne

7.   Google PageRank

Also, since we're only really working with Google here, you only need to select the Google column from the preference settings. To access preferences in Firefox for example, go to Tools > SEO Quake > Preferences then click on the "Parameters" tab. In order to access the preferences in Google Chrome you can click the SEO Quake icon, which is located to the right of the search bar on your Google Chrome browser. This will open a drop-down menu and you can enter the preferences through here.

You can of course experiment with different settings. But the seven items detailed are the most important primary pieces of information that you will need to accurately assess your ability to compete at the top of any given Google SERP. These factors involve the trust through age and trust through authority. I'll go into detail on the trust through authority in the upcoming chapters, but in order to develop any authority you need good content, so don't try to skimp on crafting excellent content for your blog's readers.

SEOquake Preferences

| General | Parameters | SERPs | Toolbar | Advanced |

Parameters

	Seobar	Toolbar	Google	Yahoo	Bing	Baidu	Yandex	Linkinfo
Google pagerr	☑	☑	☑	☑	☑	☑	☑	☑
Google indx		☑	☑		☑	☑	☑	☑	☑
Google lir				☑				
Google cacl ate								
Yahoo index								
Yahoo dir								
SEMrush links	☑	☑	☑	☑	☑	☑	☑	☑
SEMrush linkdomain		☑	☑		☑	☑	☑	☑	☑
SEMrush linkdomain2								
Bing index		☑	☑		☑	☑			☑
Dmoz								
Alexa rank		☑	☑	☑	☑	☑			☑
Webarchive age		☑	☑	☑	☑	☑			☑
Twitter Tweets		☑	☑	☑				
FaceBook likes		☑	☑	☑				
Google PlusOne		☑	☑	☑				
Whois		☑	☑		☑	☑	☑	☑	☑
Page source		☑	☑		☑	☑	☑	☑	☑
Robots.txt		☑						
Sitemap.xmi		☑						
SEMrush Rank		☑	☑		☑	☑	☑	☑	☑
SEMrush SE Traffic								
SEMrush SE Traffic price		☑	☑		☑	☑	☑	☑	☑
Delicious index								
Technorati index								
Digg index								
Domain ip								
Yandex CY								☑	
Yandex index								☑	
Yandex catalogue								☑	
Baidu index							☑		
Baidu links							☑		
Compete Rank								

| Restore default parameters ▾ | New... | Edit | Delete | Get more parameters... |

| Reset to defaults | | Close |

BRAINSTORMING KEYWORDS

Your approach to finding the right keywords for your blog articles should always start with a brainstorming session. Of course, you'll need to consider your niche and think about the general topic that you want to write about, but when you've come up with that, you can start brainstorming some ideas. If you're a pen and paper kind of person, then you should grab a notepad in hand, and if you prefer the computer, then I would suggest opening up an Excel spreadsheet. Whatever tools you choose, pick one and immerse yourself in the hunt for the right keyword for your blog post.

What you're going to be looking for, ultimately, is the primary keyword you will use on your article along with some secondary keywords. But if you recall, Google really wants you to only place relevant keywords to the content on the page so make sure you don't use secondary keywords or tags that have no relevancy to the article you intend to post. Also, I can't express enough the importance of this phase, and time well spent hunting for the right keywords will be time well saved in the future when trying to rank on SERPs for those searches.

The first thing you'll need to begin with of course, is your niche. Whether you're blogging about children's toys, cell phone accessories, weight loss products, or whatever it may be, try to analyze your industry and resultant keywords from different angles. Write down as many different ideas as you possibly can about the business, niche, industry, competitors, products, or customer demographics you intend to focus on in your blog article. This should be a good starting point for you when you start to actually analyze the amount of searches some of those terms gets compared with how competitive it is to rank for those keywords.

When brainstorming there are a few different approaches. There's a direct approach, say if you're blogging about a weight loss pill, you might simply begin with the terms "diet pills" or "weight loss pills". However, going beyond the direct approach to a specific type of product is an answer to a question such as "how to lose weight fast" or "best pills to take for fast weight loss". Now, you'll notice that some of these phrases are *long-tail keywords* that offer one of the lowest barriers to entry in SEO ranking.

As previously discussed, the long-tail keywords usually have low competition but considerably good search volumes. When approached correctly, long-tail keywords are one of the simplest types of search queries to rank first page or number one for, as you won't see as much competition for long-tail keywords as you will for shorter ones. An example of a long-tail keyword would be "how to lose weight in less then 30 days" as opposed to just "how to lose weight," or even "how to lose weight fast." The latter two terms will be harder to rank for because there will be a lot more competition.

When conducting your keyword research, keep in mind that you'll need to create unique blog content based around the keywords that you've selected, so choose wisely. Don't try to select a good keyword just because there is low competition if you don't think you'll be able to write a good enough article on it. Remember, the article or content has to be interesting, engaging and provide value.

Writing articles for short-tail keywords is a lot easier than writing articles for long-tail keywords, but it's harder to rank at the top of SERPs quicker. In retrospect, selecting a long-tail keyword may make content writing more difficult, but the ease of ranking at the top of SERPs much better. Since factors come into play when ranking a keyword, you won't actually know how well you do until your content is out there and indexed. This is part of Google's secrecy-shrouded machine. It won't show immediate results in a direct effort to confuse most people from not knowing specifically what tactics worked and what didn't.

All you really have to keep in mind is that you're going to write excellent content that is well researched from an SEO perspective. Also, if you're just starting out with your blog, Google's spiders will be visiting your blog a lot less often, so you're forced to wait longer periods of time until you can see a noticeable effect from the work you've put in. This can frustrate most bloggers, especially early on. However, if you purchase an aged domain name and do the proper work in creating authority for your blog, this process is usually sped up considerably.

The game of wait and see can be one of the most wearisome parts of the SEO business, but there's just no way around it. Until you have a blog with a high PageRank (4 or above) you won't see immediate results for ranking a keyword. You will have to wait as much as 14 to 21 days to notice the initial effects of your SEO so it's important to do it right the first time around.

RESEARCHING KEYWORDS

To begin the actual work required in performing your keyword research, take your brainstorming session ideas and head over to the Google Adwords Keyword Tool. This is where you'll begin to key in your keywords to begin the process of researching them. Access the Google Adwords Keyword Tool at https://adwords.google.com/o/KeywordTool and begin typing in your keyword ideas from your brainstorming session. You can either do the searches one by one, or you can search them all at once by separating them onto separate lines.

Let's say for example that you wanted to write a blog article on how to start a business. Now, you would have to do some brainstorming on this because simply using "how to start a business" will be too highly competitive, even though it's a long-tail keyword. The more specific you are, the likelier you will be to rank high on Google's SERPs. Especially if you have a brand-new blog and you're just starting out, go with a topic that is more specific. For example, you may want to tell people about what type of business they can start. You can use anything such as:

- How to start a daycare business

- How to start a day trading business

- How to start a Website design business

As long as you stay within your blog's niche whatever that may be, you can select any topic that provides as much specific information as possible. Aside from those that I just suggested, you can provide time-specific or price-specific information as well in order to increase the length of your long-tail keyword. For example:

- How to start a daycare business in 30 day

- How to start a day trading business with less than $1000

- How to start a Website design business with less than $100

As you'll come to find, the longer your long-tail keyword is, the easier you are going to be able to rank higher, faster. In the beginning, this should be your sole focus. As your readership on your blog expands, you can shift to short-tail keywords, but those are going to have some hefty competition. To start analyzing these keywords using the Google Adwords Keyword Tool, just key them into the search box and click on the "keyword ideas" tab as indicated in the preceding image. This will provide you with related keyword ideas to your searched keywords.

Once you conduct the search, Google will return some data related to the specific keywords that you entered in. You'll notice in the preceding image that you are given the level of competition, the global monthly searches, and the local monthly searches. The local monthly searches are only applicable if you're blogging about something that you want to have more local attention for. For example, if you're blogging about a specific shop in a certain town, you may want to pay attention to the local monthly searches. But, for the most part, you really only need to concern yourself with the global monthly searches.

In the search results produced here, you'll see that the first two keywords have high search competition, whereas the third one has nominal search competition. The hyphen indicates that the competition is nominal and you can almost always rank #1 for these types of keyword searches. However, the search volume is also going to be nominal, but it's always better to rank high on a keyword with low search volume than it is to rank on an obscure page far away from the first page on searches with high competition. As you build up trust with Google you'll be able to tackle those short-tail keywords down the road.

Another useful part of the Google Adwords Keyword Tool is that it provides keyword suggestions just underneath the box where your specific keyword results were returned are the keyword ideas. If you selected the "keyword ideas" tab, here you'll see a variety of suggestions on other keywords that may be useful to you in determining the specific blog article you intend to write. However, it's best to search for the keyword ideas with only one intended keyword, so in this case, let's re-run the keyword search using only the third keyword, which produced nominal competition.

When we re-run the search for "how to start a daycare business in 30 days," we'll get back some keyword ideas that can help narrow down our research. This search produces 800 related keyword searches all with varying competition levels so the best thing to do is to click the "competition" tab column and sort it from low to high competition. This way you can only focus on the keywords that have low competition, and those that have medium competition if you choose to. There are about 20 low competition keywords returned for this search's keyword ideas. Let's pick three of them here:

- How to start a small daycare (low competition)

- How to launch a small business (low competition)

- Running an in home daycare (medium competition)

It's also important to pay attention to the search volume, which is indicated in the "Global Monthly Searches" column. Try to go for high search volume with low competition. If you have to pick a medium competition keyword, that's okay too as we'll move onto a further analysis of just how "medium" the competition is on that keyword. However, for the most part, you'll just want to stick to low competition, but for the sake of comparison here, I've selected one medium competition keyword.

Now comes the part where we get to peer into Google's SERPs using x-ray glasses, or in another words, SEO Quake. Make sure that you have SEO quake installed now, and open the browser where you've set it up in to initiate the searches. Navigate to Google and enter each one of these keywords in one by one. As you do so, you'll notice search results that have a little toolbar underneath each listing giving you detailed information on them. The proceeding image is an example of the search results produced using the Chrome browser with the SEO Quake toolbar installed for the keyword "How to start a small daycare."

1. Checklist for Opening a **Day Care** Center - **Small Business** ...
smallbusiness.chron.com › Types of Businesses to Start › Day Care Centers ▾
Once you make a decision to **start** a **day care** center, contact your local **child care** ...
The U.S. **Small** Business Administration cautions that developing a business ...

SEOquake PR: 1 L: n/a L: 0 LD: 598177   Age: July 1, 2010   Tw: 51 I: 121 +1: 0 whois

2. Ideas to **Start** a Home **Day Care** Business - **Small Business** ...
smallbusiness.chron.com › ... › Starting a Medical Business ▾
Running a **day care** business can be emotionally rewarding and financially lucrative.
One of the hardest parts of **starting** an in-home **day care** may be the ...

SEOquake PR: 2 L: n/a L: 1 LD: 598177   Age: July 1, 2010   Tw: 51 I: 121 +1: 0 whois

3. **Starting a Child Care Business?** - Small Business Administration
www.sba.gov › ... › Newsroom › Community › For Lenders ▾
May 25, 2010 – Here is a summary of the key steps involved in **starting** a **child care** business. It also includes links to government tools and resources that can ...

SEOquake PR: 3 L: n/a L: 0 LD: 170255   Age: June 5, 1997   Tw: 2832 I: 6.6k +1: 0 whois

4. **How to start** a home day care - She Knows
www.sheknows.com/parenting/articles/.../how-to-start-a-home-day-care ▾
Feb 2, 2009 – ... perfect solution. Here's the info you need to **start** your own **daycare** at home. ... I have been running a **small daycare** for about three months.

SEOquake PR: 2 L: n/a L: 0 LD: 815398   Age: October 4, 1999   Tw: 24450 I: 2k +1: 0 whois

I've included the PageRank from Google in these searches even though Google has begun to phase this feature out as not being as important. The PageRank is Google's gauge of how important a Webpage is. It's the overall rank – out of a highest possible number of 10 and a lowest possible number of 0 – of a Webpage on the Internet. PageRank is determined by traffic volume so Websites like Facebook, Google, and YouTube all have very high PageRanks, and other Websites with low traffic can have little to no PageRank.

In the proceeding image, you'll see a graphical representation of PageRank, created by Elliance Inc., with some examples of sites that meet each PageRank. You'll notice in the graphic how Google is at the top of a very large mountain.

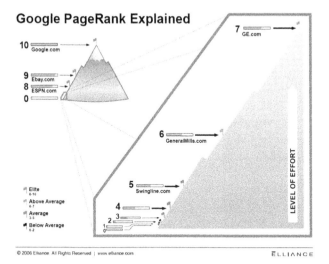

Not many sites fall between Google (PageRank 10) and GE.com (PageRank 7) and as you can see, a PageRank of 3 to 4 then to 5 are significant increases. The amount of traffic required to increase by just one PageRank at this level is exponentially greater than the level just below it. This makes an incredible difference in your ability to compete for certain keywords. As soon as the PageRank falls to a more manageable level it becomes much easier.

This is all-important because the SEO Quake toolbar can reveal some important information when it comes to PageRank and the other information used in the computation of rank by Google. In the search for "How to start a small daycare," you'll notice that the preceding image shows a PageRank of 1 for the first listing, a PageRank of 2 for the second listing, a PageRank of 3 for the third listing, and a PageRank of 2 for the fourth listing. That means that the third listing has the highest authority when it comes to Google, but it doesn't seem to appear in the #1 position. Why is that?

Well, the third listing has a very old domain age. As you can see, the domain was first registered in 1997, making it far older than the top 2 listings, which are from the same Website but only date back to 2010. What the first two listings do have is a high number of links to the domain: 598,177 links to the domain to be exact. That is an extraordinary amount of links. This far outweighs the oldest domain that's located in the #3 position, which only has 170,255 links. Only. Yes, I know, it's a lot of links. Can you see how it may be difficult to rank at the top of this search when competing? Even though this is low competition, outranking the top 4 positions is going to take a domain with some established age or some heavy backlinking to the page itself.

What you'll also notice in the top few listings is that although they all have a lot of links to their domains (indicated by the symbol "LD" in the SEO Quake toolbar), the actual links to the pages (indicated by the symbol "L" in the SEO Quake toolbar) that are ranking have 0 to 1 at the most. This could potentially mean that creating a blog article that has a lot of links to the specific page optimized for "How to start a small daycare," over and above the domain may get you ranked high. However, you will be competing with older domain names that have a lot of link juice to their domains. You might be able to rank on the first page, but it may be difficult to get in the #1 slot.

Another thing to note is that none of the listings here have the exact phrase "How to start a small daycare," within their titles. The listings that appear all use LSI, or in another words, Google is using LSI to determine the top listings here. It is possible that by creating a blog article with the exact title "How to start a small daycare," may get you ranked in the number one position, but you will have to address some of the other factors such as have a domain with some age, build some authority through linking, and have very good content. But, since the keyword "How to start a small daycare," has low competition, as we determined before, it's most certainly worth a shot.

By testing the other two keywords, you can conduct a similar analysis based upon the top few listings by using the SEO Quake toolbar. This entire process should become like second nature to you and you should never write a blog post without first having a laser-focused target keyword. If you can learn to do this, over time as each article gains rank and you build authority, the entire blog's authority will increase, but it's certainly not going to happen overnight. This type of link building effort takes time, and in fact, it must be done over an extended period of time to seem much more natural and organic.

7
BUILDING TRUST THROUGH AUTHORITY

Building trust through authority essentially means that you work on getting other Websites that Google already trusts, to link to you. This creates authority for your own blog, and when done properly it provides a significant boost in visibility to your Website as long as you don't violate any of Google's new rules. The new rules are the algorithm updates that I addressed at the beginning of this book. Google can "spook" easily, especially if your domain name is brand new and not aged so you have to tread with caution.

Building trust through authority is also know as Off-Page SEO (or Off-Site SEO), which refers to all the SEO work done away from your Website that helps it rank on Google's SERPs. Link building, social media marketing, forum posting, and blog commenting, are all examples of Off-Site SEO work and all ways that you can build trust through authority for your blog.

The primary goal for your Off-Site SEO efforts is to build up as many high quality, IP address diverse, and keyword diverse links back to your blog as possible. The linking must look completely natural and organic for you to rank high. If Google sees 10,000 backlinks with the same keyword over and over created in a very short period of time, it will know you are participating in "link schemes", considered to be a Black-Hat SEO technique and your blog will be demoted and Sandboxed.

But building trust through authority is a highly arduous task, and Off-Site SEO is an enormous undertaking. With so many changes being instituted recently by Google it seems as though at times you're walking on a tightrope trying to balance all the different tasks required while not violating any algorithm rules in place. It's not enough to just have an aged domain, unique content, good keyword density, and near perfect On-Page SEO. You have to tell the search engines that you're relevant by creating a diverse set of links bridging back to your Website.

If you think of your blog when you first launch, it's likened to a lonely little island sitting off the coast of millions of other islands and continents ranging from very small to super-sized. These surrounding landmasses are other Websites and blogs that have varying different PageRanks. It's your job to get all of these other Websites to begin linking to your own blog. This is the largest grind, or grunt work, that you'll endure when conducting Off-Page SEO work to increase your blog's trust through authority.

Getting other high PageRank Websites to create links to your own site develops this trust through authority. It's these links from high PageRank sites that create the virtual bridges that span the unending divide of Cyberspace, connecting your Website with the rest of the Internet world. But an island with no bridges is an island with no traffic, which is what your blog is likened to when it first hits the scene in Cyberspace.

You have to get to work building these virtual bridges just as soon as you begin to post your first articles on your blog. Because an island with many bridges to and from other islands has the opportunity for an exceedingly large amount of traffic. Since link relationships have a very early root in search engine rankings, these link bridges play a major role in relevancy for search results.

But developing trust through authority is not just a determination of the number of links back to your blog. You can't just set out to create an exceedingly large amount of unnatural looking links from obscure sites throughout the Web. The links that you set about creating have to be natural links that come from good content, or social media links that are shared numerous times. Otherwise, by creating unnatural links through "link schemes," you run the risk of being demoted in Google's SERPs each time they run a Google Penguin update or any other algorithm update that searches for potential SEO "cheats."

Your blog's ranking ultimately will be based on the popularity of these virtual link bridges that you create and what type of content they stem from. The best types of links are links that come from not only high PageRank Websites, but also content that is unique and optimized for SEO. This is also referred to as content marketing, or when you leverage other authority sites for the purpose of building quality content that then links back to your own blog. Also, it's important to note that one link from a very popular site like Facebook or YouTube (both have PageRank of 9 out of 10) has much more value then 10 links from very unpopular Websites with low PageRank.

The goal in Off-Site SEO is to build up as many links

as possible from as diverse of a range of Websites as possible. This link building will take up a majority of your Off-Site SEO efforts. While link building is a critical component of Off-Site SEO, too much link building in too short of a time can actually hurt you. When Google released its Google Penguin algorithm update in April of 2012, one of its sole goals was to seek out Websites that were participating in these so-called "link schemes." If it determined that a certain site went from virtually no links, to thousands of links in a very short period of time, Google's Penguin algorithm came to the conclusion that the site was participating in "link schemes". This is also part of what we call the Google Sandbox Effect that can happen not only by having a new domain name, as discussed earlier, but also by participating in these link schemes or violating any of Google's other new rules.

It's important to not only have a good quantity of links that are from high quality sites that have link diversification, but also that the links built up to your site have diversified keywords and are created gradually and not drastically in a short period of time. This may be a lot of rules to remember, but just keep in mind that you always want your efforts to be as organic looking as possible. For example, when you set about creating links to your pages, if you always use the same hyperlink or text in your links, and do this hundreds of times or thousands of times over, Google will know that you're cheating. Instead, you have to make the links look organic and natural.

Having 1,000 links created in a period of one week all with the same two or three keywords is very unnatural, even if you those links are coming from very different Websites. The key here is to have a very diversified set of keywords that includes your primary keyword, secondary keywords, and generic keywords. Once these links are created, they must be pinged slowly through a drip feed system, like the one available through http://bit.ly/linkliciousme.

For example, let's say that you have a blog article that you've posted about "best way to write a resume for the high tech industry." Well, you're going to want to have links from other sites that have this keyword phrase in it, but you will also want to have secondary links, or the LSI variation of it. For example, you may want to have links that say "how to write a resume for high tech jobs," or "best resume writing methods for jobs in high tech." What Google is looking for are links that occur naturally within posts and not ones that look unnatural. That's why these LSI links are just as important as the primary keyword links. You should also have generic links to the page that would include terms like "click here," and "check out the blog here," or "read the article at this link." These are generic links that people would normally post on blogs and comment in forums. Always remember the natural and organic approach is the best approach.

The best Grey-Hat SEO method that I've found to quicken the pace of this is to use the following service – http://bit.ly/dripfeedlinksco. They offer a phenomenal system for link building that is as close as you can get to natural and organic. You can enter your entire set of primary, LSI, and generic keywords and it will produce high quality links with those keywords in high PageRank and IP-diversified links throughout the Web. Again, nothing is going to be as natural and organic as doing the work yourself, but I have found this approach to work very well and it has been Penguin-proof but there are no guarantees that it always will. Don't be afraid to do the work yourself and get your hands dirty. But, if you don't have the time, this is certainly an excellent alternative.

While you may not understand it now, anytime you have an obsession over something and you track it on an hourly and daily basis (like some do in the SEO industry), you come to know what works and what doesn't over time and you can see major shifts clearly when they occur. It's like watching a stock on the stock market move up and down with its fluctuations as it ebbs and flows both against and with the market.

There are always factors that can be attributed to the rise and fall of a stock, and the same goes for the rise and fall of a domain name on Google's SERPs. The difficulty here is to be able to determine what works and what doesn't in a timely fashion in order to make adjustments geared around ranking you higher before Google runs its next major algorithm updates.

The issues with SEO at times are that changes may not be noticeable for two or more weeks from the date you publish a piece of content and begin conducting SEO work on it. Unless you have a very popular site that's heavily trafficked (PR 4 and above), any changes you make may take considerable time to show up as an improvement on the SERPs.

SEARCH RELEVANCY

Google's main purpose is to provide its users with the most relevant search results that it possibly can. In essence, it wants to ensure that the end user conducting his or her search finds the information that they are seeking. And in order for you to stay relevant and get your blog noticed at the top of Google's SERPs, you have to ensure that you abide by Google's rules and not try to skimp on content, or cheat your way up to the top. As long as you can write really good blog articles that are interesting, engaging and add value to the reader, and you do this with SEO in mind, your blog will increase in relevancy more and more as the weeks, months and years go by.

There's really a large push and pull going on between search engine marketers and search engines like Google. Both are striving to stay relevant. Google wants to provide the most relevant data and the search engine marketer wants to be considered the most relevant. But remember, there are only a finite number of positions on that illustrious first page, so relevancy is the big key. Because by striving to provide more and more relevant search results as the Internet becomes more crowded, Google has been forced to fine tune its algorithm many times over by rewarding those that stick to the rules, and punishing those who try to bend them.

When building your Off-Page SEO campaign to gain trust through authority, your goal should always be to look as natural and organic as possible. Google loves natural looking links that point to unique well-researched content, so use that information to your advantage by writing blog articles that are useful and unique. This foundational element of the search giant's computation has always existed and will most likely increase as time goes on so you have to approach your article writing with care. Make sure that the content is nothing short of excellent, and ensure that you've done your best to check your work for grammatical errors and spelling. Poorly written content, even if the underlying content provides value, is going to be counter-productive.

When conducting your Off-Page SEO efforts it's easy to try to rush through the process of trying to build as many links as possible in the shortest period of time simply because you feel pressured and want to achieve immediate results. But this will only backfire in your face because if Google sees the velocity of link creation throttling at the red line, your site will get penalized, especially if those links are unnatural poor-quality links. Of course, the problem is that Google doesn't tell anyone what this amount is. If they did, it would make all of our jobs easier, but simply keeping an organic frame of mind is always the best bet. Don't try to create thousands of links per week or month. Keep it natural, and make the link building creation smooth and consistent. Just don't overdo it.

If you're faced with a situation where you've created some bad links in the past and you're unable to remove them yourself, you must disavow those links with Google. When you disavow a link, you tell Google not to count that link in its algorithm. You can find a sampling of links to your site by typing the following into the Google search engine: [link:www.yourdomain.com] where you would replace *yourdomain.com* with your own domain of course. If you've found poor quality links head to http://bit.ly/disavowtool, which is located on the Google Webmaster Tools site, and you can begin the process of disavowing low-quality links to your blog.

I've been faced with countless situations where clients went out and built links too fast and fed them to Google too quickly and were quickly flagged. However, while they were building the links their Website was moving up the rankings so they didn't think twice about it. But that's the trick up Google's sleeve because when it runs its Penguin updates these days it happens only every so often. When it does, it sends shockwaves through the Web, and those who were violating Google's Webmaster Guidelines get quickly penalized, while those who were abiding by its rules, move up in the rankings.

Don't allow yourself to fall victim to this trap. I can't repeat this enough because this is a major pitfall that new and existing SEO individuals are faced with time and time again. Be diligent and methodical in your link building efforts but don't try to forcibly overdo it. And the more time you take and effort you put into building a solid Off-Page and On-Page SEO foundation for your blog, the better the rewards will be. Consistently writing unique well-researched blog articles with natural and organic looking inbound links to them should always be your primary concern.

The more relevant your overall page is to the keyword

being searched, the more likely you'll rank at the top. For example, it will be difficult to rank an investment article high on a blog that has its primary topic of discussion as celebrity news. Of course there are some exceptions to the rule such as just how popular that site housing the article is, but for the most part, try to ensure that your keyword is relevant to your site-wide topic or niche.

Over time, as you work on SEO for specific pages and boost each page respectively, it will help the collective group increase in SERP rankings. Since these pages will most likely share tags or categories that create a linked relationship between them, this will result in the collective rise of the domain's search engine visibility along with its pages and articles as well.

PINGING

It's not enough that you have to go out and create this complex and vast array of backlinks that link back to your blog, but in order to get Google to crawl and find them you have to do something called pinging. Since some of the sites that you'll be obtaining backlinks to your blog from will have low PageRank or no PageRank, and Google may never actually crawl those pages if you don't tell it to.

It's estimated that Google only crawls about 5% of the Web that houses low PageRank and no PageRank sites. Without any directive to go index a page with a low or no PageRank, Google spiders may never end up visiting it and your hard work in creating those links will go to waste, since they will never get indexed.

Pinging is a task that you're going to need to get used to doing each time you create an array of links back to your blog. There are two different types of pinging services that you'll be using here. The first is a pinging service for your page's URLs that you create and build over time. This type of pinging will essentially instruct

Google to visit the page on a periodic basis that you've established such as every 3 to 10 days.

Each time you post a Webpage or blog article, you need to ensure that it gets pinged on a regular basis by using a service like Pingler.com, which will ping Google spiders to visit any link on a periodic basis (from every 3 days to every 10 days). If you have content that gets updated regularly you should set this to every 3 days, and if it's less often you can pick any other day up to and between 10 days.

In addition to ensuring that your own content gets pinged, you'll also need to ensure that any mass amounts of backlinks that are created are pinged as well. If you decide to use the link building service http://bit.ly/dripfeedlinksco then you'll want to utilize a service like http://bit.ly/linkliciousme that will allow you to drip feed link pings. Drip-feeding allows you to create a larger group of links that you can then ping to Google automatically at a set rate that you determine. This should be anywhere from 10 to 40 links per day for a brand new blog, even if you have an aged domain. Keeping the number at the lower end of the spectrum will probably be a better idea. Remember, this is where you have to be careful because sending too many links (especially unnatural ones) to Google at once can get you penalized. Again this is a Grey-Hat SEO method so tread with caution if you decide to go down this route.

Pinging is very important, since your grueling efforts of creating these backlinks takes time, you want to ensure it's time well spent because without pinging those links they may never get discovered and your blog will never get credit for those backlinks.

BACKLINKING

Backlinking is one of the largest undertakings that you'll be involved in when engaged in the practice of your daily SEO efforts, aside from the actual blog writing itself. Backlinks are an essential part of any SEO campaign and it's a major weighing factor in the overall search engine algorithm that ranks your blog's importance and relevancy. When Google first launched its search engine, it started with the underlying theory that the number of backlinks created rankings. The more backlinks you had the more relevant your site was. Of course that has morphed significantly with the addition of many of the factors that I've covered in this book, but backlinks still remains as one of the core principles to placement on SERPs.

So, you're probably wondering to yourself how many backlinks you're going to need in order to rank your blog articles high up on Google's SERPs. Well, there really isn't any clear answer to that and it's going to fluctuate based on your competition for any given keyword. But your goal really is to simply ensure that you build as many natural and organic links back to your blog as you possible can over time. As I discussed in the Keyword Research chapter, it's important to understand the competition in order to be able to "snipe" your way to the top of Google. This is going to be done by using tools such as the SEO Quake plugin and the Google Keyword Tool along with any other keyword analysis tools you may decide to invest in during your blog writing and SEO career.

While understanding your competition and the number of backlinks that they have is important, you should set your sights on building as many high quality, diversified backlinks on a consistent basis as possible. The backlinks will need to be drip-fed to Google in a manner that seems organic and not as though you are paying to build these links or participating in a "link scheme".

There are a few important guidelines when it comes to backlinking that you should keep in mind. While the magnitude of backlinks is important, it's also important to understand that the "link juice" coming from a Website with a high PageRank such as YouTube will be much greater than several backlinks coming from lower PageRank sites (such as forum comments, blog posts, etc.). Aiming towards quality as opposed to quantity will get you much further in boosting link juice for your site.

Creating backlinks from popular social media profile pages is one excellent way to begin your link building campaign. Sites like Facebook, Twitter, and Google Plus are excellent starting points for any such efforts. Begin with your profile pages on the big three social media sites, and continue on to setting up profiles and dropping your site's link on authority sites as well.

To start out, simply logon to any of the sites in the proceeding list. If you already have an account, great, then you won't need to set one up. If you don't have an account, then set one up, and as soon as you do, create a link back to your own Website in your profile on that particular site.

- Blinklist.com

- Delicious.com

- Diigo.com

- Deviantart.com

- Facebook.com

- Folkd.com

- Friendfeed.com

- Hi5.com

- Identi.ca

- Jumptags.com

- Kaboodle.com

- Karmalynx.com

- Kippt.com

- LinkedIn.com

- LinksaGoGo.com

- Livejournal.com

- MyAOL.com

- Myspace.com

- Netlog.com

- Newsvine.com

- Pheed.com

- Pintrest.com

- Plurk.com

- Plus.Google.com

- Reddit.com

- Scoop.it

- Serpd.com

- Skyrock.com

- Slashdot.com

- Sonico.com

- Springpad.com

- Stumbleupon.com

- Tagged.com

- Twitter.comTypepad.com

- Vk.com

- Webshare.com

- Xing.com

- Zootool.com

Now, the best approach to doing this is to actually split the list apart and do one or two profiles each day, then ping Google and let it know where to go to index the profile page so that it can log the link that you've created in your favor. If you do them all at once, you still shouldn't have a problem, but the best fully organic approach is to split the list apart and do it little by little, informing Google by pinging it the URL each step of the way. Or, you can do all URLs, but then set them up in a drip feed if you don't feel like doing a couple each day.

Beyond the Authority Profile Pages

Once you've tackled the profile page links, the next important step to building authority is by having other very high PageRank Websites, linking to you through unique content. This is going to require some work on your behalf, but these sites are incredibly popular authority sites that anyone can post content to.

Be prepared to begin blogging and writing unique, well-researched articles that are at least 500 words that contain links back to your own blog, on these authority sites. Now, although you are already doing this on your own blog, you have to also do this on authority blogs as well. Both Webpages (the one on your Website and the one on the authority Website) should both have separate unique content about the same primary keyword. When this happens, Google automatically thinks that your content is much more relevant and important because another very good piece of content that has been optimized for a certain keyword is linking to your own blog's content optimized for that same keyword.

For example, let's just say that your unique blog article is about the top 10 ways to earn money online. After you've written this article and optimized it on your own blog, you would create another article about the top 10 ways to earn money online, but this time you would do it on an authority Website. However, the article on the authority Website would link to the article on your Website using your primary keyword. This would build instant authority because you have an important Website on the Internet with a high PageRank, linking to your own content and both are optimized for the same keyword.

This method works extremely well when both articles are highly optimized for SEO, but not over optimized. Remember not to try to go overboard when you're conducting your optimization efforts. The proceeding image is a graphical representation of what this would look like. The arrow indicates that the link is traveling from the authority site to your blog.

Content Marketing

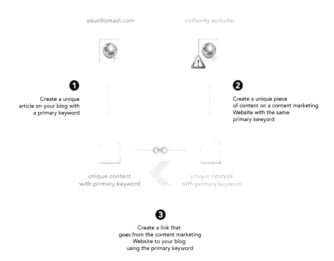

Here is a list of the authority Websites that you can begin creating content on immediately. You should of course, also create links on your profile page on these Websites as well. Aside from that, you can build content on each of these very high PageRank Websites. YouTube is the only site that you will be able to create video presentations on but that is also one of the most effective ways to begin building content.

- Squidoo.com

- Tumblr.com

- Wordpress.com

- Slideshare.com

- HubPages.com

- Scribd.com

- YouTube.com

Proceeding with Caution

One important thing to note here is that when creating links from sites like authority sites, it's easy to go overboard. What does this mean? It's easy to go out there, get very excited about your site and start spamming a ton of links within moments of each other through all of the social media sites available. This is not a good thing.

It's okay to take one article or one piece of content from your site and share it across as many different platforms as possible. However, don't do this for multiple articles each day. As much as you think you will be helping your site, you may in fact be hindering it by over posting. This is something that the Google Penguin targeted and it's something that you need to be aware of.

Sometimes in the wake of these new Google SEO rules, you're going to feel like you're walking a bit of a tight rope because you are. You don't want to overdo it or you'll end up in the Sandbox and that's not where you want to be, especially if you already have an aged domain. Take it easy with the posting and allow it to happen naturally and organically. Post a few articles or content each week and share each of those as much as possible. After a few months pass, increase your velocity of posting and linking, and repeat. This gradual increase in content, and backlinks will help you the most.

I will be discussing some techniques to use some syndication services that are available for sharing your content across different social media networks automatically in the next chapter. For now, just keep in mind that everything you do should be done as naturally and organically as possible to not rock the boat. This holds especially true if your site has no links to it when you start out.

Google keeps track of all of these things along with your link acceleration – or the pace at which the number of links that you have increases each month. Basically, Google keeps track of everything related to your site, all the time. It's like Big Brother watching over you now so be aware of that and always keep it in the back of your mind.

8
SOCIAL MEDIA STRATEGIES

With the explosive growth of social media networks like Facebook, Twitter & Google Plus, social media has not only become an important component of our lives, it has also become critical to the success of any SEO campaign. We use social media everyday to connect with the people we love and care about, and watch people's lives play out on the screen in front of us. For some, social media plays such an important role in their lives that nearly everything they do is documented from either their home computer or mobile device.

Google has of course taken notice of this explosive growth, not only by launching its own social media platform called Google Plus, but also now by beginning to give weight to social media likes, shares, and tweets more than ever before. While the weight that Google gives for each share on various different social networks is unknown, it is clear that it is providing more prominence for pages & sites that have heavy shares through the social media realm. This "Social Rank" is evidenced by the data garnered from the SEO Quake toolbar because as you use it to research keywords you will notice domains that don't have a lot of links but have a lot of shares for that particular listing or blog post related to the keyword search, ranks above those with lots of links.

If you haven't already done so then it's important to setup a Facebook Page, Twitter Account, and Google Plus account for your blog in order to start garnering page likes and shares through the social media world. Even if you already have a personal account on these social networks, set one up for your blog as well. This would include setting up a dedicated Fan or Business Page on Facebook, a dedicated Fan Page or Business Page on Google Plus, and a separate Twitter account for your blog.

Social media shares are important because they come from real human people clicking on a link saying that they either liked something or wanted to share it with the rest of the world. Getting someone to like or share a page sometimes isn't that easy, especially if it involves a bland or dry topic. It's become increasingly important to get people to share and like your content, whatever it may be, due to the impact these very powerful high PageRank backlinks have in terms of Off-Site SEO link juice.

Of course most people already have a Facebook account and Twitter account, but if you're one of the few that doesn't' have these, then it's important to get this setup right away. Besides for these two social networks, having a Google Plus account is critical now as well.

There are hundreds of social media platforms out there today that have taken the term Web 2.0 to a whole new level, and Google is starting to take notice. It's also become increasingly clear by the high PageRank of some of these sites, just how popular they have become. When managing an effective SEO campaign one of the hats you are going to have to wear will be the Social Media hats.

While managing and sharing content through 3 sites may sound overwhelming, try doing it on dozens of sites at a time. There are ways, however, that you can automate some of this work. Of course, this would become virtually impossible to manage after a while. For this, reason, it's important to engage in content syndication, discussed in the following section, which will ease some of the workload here.

CONTENT SYNDICATION

One of the best, most effective strategies that you can use to begin syndication of your content on social media networks is to use the power of the tribe. Whenever working and collaborating with others in this field (and other marketing fields), group efforts always trump individual efforts. You know how the saying goes, "there's no i in team", and it certainly holds true here.

Going about syndicating your content is difficult without the power of a tribe and automatic content syndication platforms. **Tribepro**, which you can locate at the following URL http://bit.ly.com/thepowerofthetribe provides an excellent syndication platform for sharing your content amongst hundreds, if not thousands of people in your tribe. The system offers its members a unique platform to be able to quickly syndicate content and build up heavy high PageRank backlinks almost instantaneously.

Tribepro requires a membership fee and also requires that you have a subscription to Onlywire, which you can find at the following URL -

http://bit.ly/onlywiresyndication. Onlywire is a service that provides the actual syndication pipeline used by Tribepro. While this can get moderately costly, it's probably one of the best investments that you can make in the SEO industry, allowing you to quickly and effectively build very high PageRank backlinks to your blog articles through a simple interface.

Content syndication can also be placed on autopilot with Tribepro. By adding your RSS feed to the site, it will automatically feed the content from your blog into the tribe on a daily basis. This is a terrific hands-free approach to doing a major part of your SEO tasks and means that you can concentrate much more heavily on blogging, then allowing your content to flow and syndicate out into the Web on its own.

Another great way to syndicate your content for free is by using a site called EmpireAvenue.com. Empire Avenue is an excellent resource for bringing together all of your social media platforms into one place and allowing you to collaborate with other like-minded marketers that are using social media to spread and share each other's content. On Empire Avenue you can connect any number of social networks that you are participating in to the service and begin collaborating with other online marketers working to boost their SEO and social media shares.

As a tradable commodity, your account on Empire Avenue becomes a fictitious stock on the site, earning you the Website's own currency called Eaves when your shares are purchased. While it's a fictional trading platform, the site is excellent for collaborating and doing missions with other people to either share their content or have them share yours in exchange for Eaves.

Empire Avenue is a free site, however you can always purchase more Eaves when you run dry or just do missions to earn them for free. This is an excellent way to get real human people to collaborate with, Facebook Share, like, Google Plus One, and Re-Tweet your content, all excellent sources of SEO link juice.

SOCIAL MEDIA MARKETING

One of the biggest changes to the Web over the past several years has been the emergence of social media, and its effect on SEO has been a considerable one. And although Google's algorithm is not all about the social media activity of a given piece of Web content or blog article, it is a very important aspect of it. That's why paying attention to social media and ensuring that your blog articles have a solid presence in social media is extremely important.

Because social media plays such a large role in our lives, and now in the brains of Google's algorithms, it's important that you focus on social media, and strategies that are effective for your blog in order to boost your visibility when it comes to SEO. Aside from implementing the content syndication strategies that I've recommended through various online services like TribePro and EmpireAvenue, you have to implement a solid social media strategy for your blog in order to create raving fans that will help you increase your blog's presence on the Web. The higher your "Social Rank" is, the more likely your blog posts will sore to the top of Google's SERPs each time they're posted.

So What Works?

Ever logon to Facebook (or any other social media network for that matter) and seen someone over sharing again and again? You know the one I'm talking about right? That one person amongst your group of friends, or someone you follow, who's constantly cheerleading their own work or causes. Yes, we've all come across these types of people in the past before but it's important to take a look at sharing on social media to see just what works.

You need to take a look at this and analyze it as though you were the person watching yourself share the information. You need to be on the outside looking in. How would you feel if you saw a link to the content that you just provided? Would you be inclined to click on it? Would it excite you enough to share it? Are you sharing too often?

When you ask yourself the right questions and look at the underlying blog content that you're sharing it's easy to see whether or not something is going to get traction in social media or not. Your goal of course is to get that content shared as much as possible, but how do you do this? Well, first of all, you have to have a solid base of people in your immediate inner circle to start with. If you have 1,000 friends, people in your circle or followers, it will be much easier getting traction on your social media shares than if you only had say 100 of the same.

However, aside from having a large base of fans,

followers or friends, for social media sharing to really work you have to ensure that you are adhering to the five principles of interaction. No matter what you are sharing, whether it's a photo, a video, a blog article, literally anything, the purpose of your interaction on social media is to attract, engage, connect, convert then retain.

You want to be able to create raving super fans that will help to tout your blog to their own friends. But, this doesn't happen overnight. Of course you blog has to be interesting, engaging, and provide a lot of value. But aside from that, creating a social media strategy requires consistent and concerted daily effort on your part. It's going to take time to create a base of super raving fans that will help boost your blog's visibility on SEO. You have to put in the time to make sure that you are interacting with people to create, nurture and grow your circle of followers, friends and fans.

#1 – ATTRACT

In order to draw people into your shared blog content, you have to be able to first attract them. This attraction can happen in many different ways, but you have to understand some basic principles of marketing through attraction for this to work.

The art of attracting people through social media means that their eyes have to pass the scan test. As people scan through their social media feeds they are quickly going from one status or tweet to another seeing which one catches their eyes. They are scanning.

When people scan they are scanning titles for something that pops out at them. This is where your ability in writing effective blog titles comes into play. If you have a blog title that can attract someone enough to pass the eye scan test, then you know that you've done a good job with your title. You have to think about what you yourself would click on. Is your article's title compelling enough?

Does it make you want to click? You really have to spend a good amount of time crafting a well-written title that also has your primary keyword in it.

The attraction is the key, because if people aren't attracted to what you've written, and the title isn't compelling enough, people won't click on it. For this reason, your blog will fail the eye scan test.

#2 – ENGAGE

Once you've attracted someone to your blog post you need to be able to engage them for long enough to hold their attention. Remember, no one wants to just read some plain old boring article. It has to be interesting and engaging and they need to be able to learn something or take something of value away from it.

The best way that you're going to be engaging to your friends or followers on social media is to share your content through the power of storytelling. If you are a good storyteller, then you will find this very easy and if you are not, well, this will be much more difficult. But, this is certainly a skill you can develop with practice.

Simply put, people just don't want to hear about another blog post touting some business or another affiliate program. They would rather hear a story, and if that story happens to relate to the business or affiliate program touted in your blog post, then you will hold their very fleeting attention span that much longer.

Why do you think people are so infatuated with television and the movies? It's because people love to be entertained and engaged. They want an escape from the drudgery of work and business for the most part. If you are not engaging and entertaining you will quickly lose people's interest and no one will want to read your article let alone share it.

Tell a Story

People love stories. For that reason, when you share on a platform like Facebook, Twitter, or Google Plus, make sure that you tell a story. Aside from having a blog or post title that will attract, you need to engage in order to keep them there. Whether you are sharing a photo, a video, or a link to the article on your blog, back it up with a story and make sure that your content is in line with the story.

For example, I have a close friend, Erica, who is a professional resume writer for corporate executives and she told me this story about how she wanted to advertise her services through Facebook with her blog but didn't want to come off so "salesy." She lamented to me that she hated seeing people fervently pitching their businesses around the clock and she didn't want to be "that person," as she put it.

I told my friend that she should tell a story, so I dug a little deeper and started asking her some questions about her work and whether or not she could think of any interesting stories that came to mind. She told me she did have one recent interesting story about a lady named Rosie that came to her after 10 years of working for the same company, with the desire to get her resume polished to hunt for a new job.

Rosie had an incredibly low morale at her, then present employer, because her department was merged with another department, and her new department head was someone who she had a past history of not getting along with.

Erica went on to tell me the story about how Rosie's manager had done just about everything to undermine her over the past 10 years of working at the company. Finally, this manager had begun to purposefully park in Rosie's parking spot, which was a considerably shorter walk to the office than her own. This was the final straw for Rosie apparently.

Once Erica had finished telling me the story, I told her that she could easily take Rosie's dilemma, and potentially change her name if she had to, then spin it into a blog post as a story about her resume writing services. Within this blog post, she would of course have to ensure that she optimized it for her keywords but also that she effectively told Rosie's story in a manner that would engage and entertain.

Once I had finished explaining all of this to Erica, she immediately became excited by the possibility of that story and how she could turn it into an excellent article that also provided some resume writing tips as well. I of course told her that was an excellent idea and just smiled.

I did however add one piece of information to Erica's arsenal for the story and informed her that once she finished telling the story she needed a call to action. This call to action would help to achieve the second to last principle for social media marketing: convert.

#3 – CONNECT

Connecting with your audience is one of the key principles in social media marketing. Once you've been able to attract and engage them, you have to be able to connect because that connection is the true meaning of social networking. Anytime you're able to deeply connect and affect people through your engaging stories, you will captivate your audience enough to have them become loyal fans and followers.

What some people forget at times, that are trying to use social networking solely for profit, is that connection is at the root level of its interaction. If you are unable to establish a connection, you will lose your audience. What does this mean? Well, connecting can be done in very many ways but really it means to bring out the human side in you.

People like to interact and connect with other real people. Even if you're blogging for business or profit, you have to bring the real you out and into the open. Allow people to see the more human side of you by talking about your family, placing pictures of your kids playing sports, or a million other things that can be done to show people a glimpse into the real you.

If you're telling good stories, this connection can happen fluidly within the story itself. It's your goal to always create that connection because that connection is the very fiber of the strings that will keep that fan in tact.

#4 – CONVERT

At the end of telling Rosie's story, I told Erica she needed a call to action. I told her she could use the call to action as a way to help encourage people to share the story, make someone like her page or tweet it, or as a call to visit her services page where people could purchase one of her professional resume writing packages.

Having a call to action is imperative in any blog post you put out there. Some people forget or completely leave out the call to action because they think that it is obvious that if a person is reading a blog post that has a Facebook or Twitter share button that they don't need to ask the reader to share the post. You do need to ask the reader to share the post and there's absolutely nothing wrong with doing so.

The call to action is a signal to the brain. It may be a conscious signal but often times it is an unconscious signal. By having a sentence that asks the reader to share the blog post now, you are extending the literal call to action by telling them what to do next. You will be surprised at just how well this will work.

Other ways of placing calls to action would be to use similar terms for an urge to share. For example, instead of coming out and saying, "please share," you could have a sentence that says, "By sharing this article you can help spread value to others looking for this type of information." You'll be surprised at just how well this works.

#5 – RETAIN

Once you have people as fans, followers, and blog readers, you have to be able to retain them. So many people get caught up in writing new blog posts that they forget to implement practices that would help retain their existing base of fans.

Today, in the overcrowding Web 3.0 economy, people don't want to be part of something that isn't active or interesting. If people have joined you by either following you or becoming a fan of your blog, keep them interested. Implement the three E's of retention:

1. Educate

2. Entertain

3. Empower

This requires consistent work on your behalf so make sure that you set aside time in your schedule to dedicate to your social media activities. Try to limit yourself to an hour or two each day and don't allow yourself to get too sucked in or carried away. If you have a problem overindulging in social networking, find a way to cut yourself off at a certain time. Set an alarm for yourself if you have to.

BUILDING A FAN BASE

When I talk about building a fan base, I'm of course referring to platforms like Facebook and Google Plus, which allow you to setup a page for your business, then invite people to join that page by liking it or adding it to their circles.

To most people, when they think about building a fan base, they immediately think about inviting every single friend that they have to like the page simply because they are friends. I would highly discourage you from doing this. When you try to actively promote your blog to friends in this manner, people get annoyed. You have to put yourself in their shoes. How do you feel when you get an invite from your friend to like a page? Usually you probably ignore it unless it is somehow relevant to the conversation.

Relevancy – that's the name of the game isn't it? In the Web 3.0 economy everyone is vying to be relevant. Since Google has now changed the rules, people are clamoring at every possible tidbit of information that they can devour in order to try to stay one step ahead of the curve. However, what most people end up doing is simply over self-promoting their blogs, in turn detracting more people than they attract.

In order to attract people you need to make sure that you setup a system for that attraction. You have to have an excellent piece of content loaded and ready to fire. Even better, if you have an automatic gun filled with dozens of rounds of excellent blog content just waiting on the ready to be fired, you can actively promote and gain traction to your blog's fan page without people turning a sour face. Why is that?

People simply enjoy good content that is presented in an engaging manner. If you can tell a story through the content, or relate the content to a story that provides a real sense of who you are, people will keep coming back for more.

What you want to try to do when you're interacting with people on Facebook is to not only create a fan base, but to create "super fans." What's a super fan? A super fan is not only someone who has given you their basic details as a fan, but they have also purchased from you and got another fan to purchase something from you as well. They are your biggest cheerleaders.

So how do you go about getting potential fans to become super fans? Well, it all has to do with your ability to adhere to the principle of engaging. If you are very good at engaging then you will create super fans but it won't happen overnight. Super fans are nurtured and created over an extended period of time of sharing. If you want to create super fans, here are some of the basic strategies that you need to adhere to when you are engaging on social networks like Facebook:

#1 – The Human Element

People like to interact with other real people on social networks and if they find that you like to come out from behind your business and show your true self through shares about your personal life, you will create much deeper and lasting connections. You can create the human element in your engagements by taking 1 in every 5 posts that you post and making it a personal post.

For example, maybe your son just scored a goal at his school's soccer game and you decide to share that, or maybe, your daughter just got her first straight A report card and you decide to share that. Maybe even, if you're having a bad day share that. As long as whatever you share can be shared with tact and can engage and bring out the human element of the man or woman behind the scenes, you will create a deeper and more lasting connection.

#2 – Become an Authority

No matter what your niche is, becoming an authority will set you apart from the rest of blogs out there in the world. There are so many fan pages and business pages out there that post nonsense that in order to set yourself apart you need to post about topics of interest in your industry and niche.

If you have to, setup a Google News Alert so that you hear about trending topics first, then share these with your fans and followers. After a while, people will begin to recognize that you are a true authority in the industry and that they hear the important news about what's going on in your niche first, from you.

#3 – Encourage Fan Dialog

After you post on Facebook, or any other social network for that matter, stick around for a little while to create a dialog with your fans or followers. Just think about a real life situation: if you were speaking to a friend, would you say something then walk away? Probably not, unless you were in a fight, but on Facebook, stick around and encourage a two-way dialog with your followers.

The more you encourage dialog with your fans, the more you will keep them interested and interacting. This is key to nurturing fans into super fans. You want to create a good level of interaction that doesn't have them forgetting that you even exist but also doesn't have you overdoing it. Create a back and forth and allow the dialog to come naturally, don't try to force it.

When you create dialog and make a post active on Facebook, it encourages fans to share that post. If that post happens to have a link to your blog for an article that you wrote, then this will be counted in Google's algorithm for search visibility. This is considered an authority link since Google trusts Facebook's Website and any links or shares coming from it have a high factor towards your visibility.

If you post interesting and engaging posts, then you are encouraging shares, which will eventually lead to more visibly on Google. Can you see how the simple act of telling an engaging story with a link to your Website can benefit you in more ways than one?

#4 – Spreading the Word

There's no better promotion than word-of-mouth promotion. In order to get fans talking about your blog or your company and spreading the word, you have to create giveaways. By creating giveaways you begin to invite interest and interaction through a much higher level than your standard interaction.

You can setup a system to reward your fans or followers who invite their friends to your content or giveaway through apps on Facebook such as the Wildfire app - http://www.wildfireapp.com. By setting a system for reward, you will further encourage your existing fan base to spread the word for you.

#5 – Track & Analyze

Of course, no true SEO marketer's work is complete until they are able to successfully measure the fruits of their labor. Get in the habit of tracking and analyzing your activities on social networks. Since you have the tools to track your blog and keyword activity by using Google Analytics and Google Webmaster Tools, you also want to be able to track the social activity for your blog posts as well. Facebook provides an array of tools to do this with, however, there are other third party tools as well.

You can use a Website like Topsy – http://www.topsy.com - to gain instant social insight or you can check out any of the other following Websites as well:

- http://www.socialbakers.com

- http://www.socialmention.com
- http://klout.com
- http://www.twitterfall.com
- http://www.hootsuite.com
- http://friendorfollow.com
- http://blekko.com

OTHER BOOKS IN THIS SERIES

If you enjoyed this book on SEO, I would really appreciate it if you could take a few moments and share your thoughts by posting a review on Amazon. You can visit the Amazon page at the following URL: http://www.amazon.com/dp/B00CQOJJGY

I put a lot of care into the books that I write and I hope that this care and sincerity come across in my writing because in the end I write to bring value to other people's lives. I hope that this book has brought some value to your life. I truly do.

Also, feel free to also take a look at some of the other books in this series entitled: *The SEO Series* available for sale on Amazon. The following titles can also be found that I have authored:

- *SEO White Book – The Organic Guide to Google Search Engine Optimization - http://www.amazon.com/dp/B00BUOPFHI*

- *SEO Simplified – Learn Search Engine Optimization Strategies and Principles for Beginners - http://www.amazon.com/dp/B00BN7PGEY*

- *The SEO Black Book – A Guide to the Industry's Secrets - http://www.amazon.com/dp/B00B7GIVSE*

I wish you all the best in your SEO educational pursuits.

All the Best,

R.L. Adams

APPENDIX
SEO TERMINOLOGY

Aged Domains – An aged domain is a domain that has been in indexed by Google at least two or more years ago and it's a critical component of any successful SEO campaign. Google penalizes new domain names, making it very difficult to rank any keywords at the #1 position or even on the first page of search results for that matter in the beginning. Purchasing or having an aged domain will be one of the critical factors in your success for ranking a site high for any given keyword.

ALT tags – Also known as alternative tags, these are the tags that appear within the HTML <img> tags that present the alternate data to the search engines to provide a description of what the image is. For optimal search engine rankings you should have at least one image ALT tag that correlates with your site or page's primary keyword.

Backlinking – Likely to be your biggest undertaking when it comes to SEO, backlinking is the effort involved with creating hyperlinks that link back to your Website.

Black-Hat SEO – Black-Hat SEO is a term used to describe a SEO tactics that are not compliant with Google's Webmaster Guidelines. Black-Hat SEO techniques are frowned upon by the search engine industry. Examples of Black-Hat SEO techniques are trying to hide keywords within HTML comment tags or trying to cloak pages.

Breadcrumb – A navigational aid used on Websites, breadcrumbs not only allow users to quickly jump through informational sections on the site, they also provide high SEO value by allowing the search engine spiders access to quickly navigate and spider through a site, indexing data faster and more efficiently.

Cloaking – This is a technique that delivers different content to the search engine spiders then it does to real human visitors. The cloaking technique is oftentimes used to mask the real content or change the real content of a page and make it appear differently to a search engine spider. This is considered a Black-Hat SEO technique and while it is sometimes used for legitimate purposes, it is oftentimes used to display pornographic material to real human visitors while only displaying non-pornographic material to a search engine spider.

CPC – Cost-per-click, or CPC, is a term used in online

paid advertising to indicate click through percentages. The cost per click is calculated by diving the number of clicks with the total amount spent on the advertisement. For example, if you spent $100 on an ad and 200 clicks was received; the CPC would be $0.50 cents.

CSS – Cascading Style Sheets, also known as CSS, is a style sheet presentation markup language that is used to position elements, layouts, colors, fonts, images, and construct a Web page on the whole. While CSS is used primarily in styling HTML Web pages, it is also used to style XML and other documents.

Dofollow Links – Dofollow links are an attribute associated with an HTML hyperlink that tell a search engine to continue to link through to the site, disseminating some of the site's important link juice. These are very powerful types of links that work well when pointed to your site or to a link pyramid that leads to your site. When a search engine sees a Dofollow link they continue linking through to the site, passing part of the SEO link juice that would have been offered to that page had the link been a Nofollow link.

Duplicate Content – In the search engine world, content is king, but duplicate content is the court jester. Copying large chunks of content to your site is one of the biggest no-nos in the industry. The search engines will figure it out sooner or later and you will be demoted in the rankings. If you're going to do SEO right, make sure all the content is high-quality and unique content that's well researched.

Headings – HTML headings are blocks of code that are placed around certain words, styling and providing a certain level of prominence in the overall page structure. Heading tags range from <h1> through <h6>, however, in the modern SEO world the first three hold the most importance. Tags <h1> through <h3> should all contain the primary keyword spaced throughout the page with the <h1> and <h2> tags being above the Website fold.

Internal Link – Internal links are links from your page's content to another page or section on the same domain. Internal links are important when it comes to On-Site SEO.

Keyword – A keyword is a word or phrase that is used to optimize a Website or Webpage. Selecting keywords is one of the most important tasks in SEO work and selecting the right keywords in the outset can either make or break you. It's important to note that the keyword "Miami vacation" and "vacation Miami" will produce different search results, so the order and positioning of the words within the phrase is just as important.

Keyword Density – The keyword density is the number of times a keyword appears on a page in relation to the total number of words. Optimal keyword density ranges from 2% to 5% with anything considerably over 5% being construed as SPAM and anything considerably lower then 2% being construed as not keyword rich enough and thus less relevant. It's important when writing your content that your primary keyword is evenly distributed throughout the page, making sure that it appears in the first and last sentence of the content as well as evenly spaced throughout the balance of the words.

Keyword Stuffing – Keyword stuffing is the over usage of a keyword in content or meta keyword tags, something that used to be popular many years ago, but is now frowned upon as a Black-Hat SEO technique. Keyword stuffing is achieved in various different ways which include placing the phrase multiple times within the Meta tags while combined with other words in different combinations, applying the same color to the keywords as the background making them invisible, using the <noscript> tag, and using CSS z-positioning. All of these practices will get you demoted and sometimes de-indexed by search engines like Google.

Long Tail Keyword – A long tail keyword is a keyword that has a minimum of at least 3 words and any maximum number of words. Long tail keywords are used by marketers trying to target a specific niche, question or topic, which produce near similar results to a broader search term of lessor keywords but may have higher competition. Long tail keywords are a great way to rank at the top of search engine results for terms that may otherwise be more difficult to rank for.

Link Bait – Link Bait refers to content that is created in order to garner as many links to it as possible. Since backlinks are one of the primary drivers of SERP positioning, many SEO efforts include the creation of content with the primary goal to get as many links back to that content as possible.

Link Farm – A link farm is a group of sites that all hyperlink to one another, back and forth in an oscillating fashion. While link farms used to be advantageous, they don't have large relevancy today since the two-way links make it confusing for search engines to determine which site is the vendor and which is the promoting site.

Link Juice – This is the SEO linking power of a page and usually refers to the combined sum of the link power of all the pages linking into it. You'll hear the term link juice referenced when quantifying the power of a certain link or a page that those links lead to.

Link Pyramid – A Link Pyramid is a very powerful form of Off-Site SEO backlinking that involves the creation of a linking structure that is extremely powerful. Think of the strength in physical form that a real pyramid has and how the transference of force is physically supported by the structure itself and how that has stood the test of time. Link Pyramids generally have three tiers: a bottom tier with low level links, a middle with medium level links, and a top level with high level EDU, GOV or other authority links. The bottom links link to the middle, the middle links link to the top, and the top links link to your site.

Link Sculpting – When you implement attributes to links to affect their behavior in how search engines interpret them, you're engaging in link sculpting. The most common form of link sculpting is using the Nofollow or Dofollow link sculpting forms. The Nofollow links tell a search engine not to follow a link, thus leaving the link juice on the page, while a Dofollow link tells a search engine to continue on to follow that link thus disseminating the link juice to the next page.

Link Wheel – A Link Wheel is a form of linking that links one site to another while also linking back to your site as well. The links flow in a sort of wheel format with the spokes being links back to your site in the center. When done correctly, a link wheel can be a powerful form of SEO boost for your Website and the most effective forms of link wheels are organically fashioned ones that utilize social media platforms as their linking mediums.

Meta Keywords – Meta keywords are part of a set of Meta Tags that appear in the header of Websites. Meta keywords used to be prominently used in search engine rankings but have no interpreted value of importance today. Instead of using meta keywords, search algorithms now use other tags such as heading tags, site content, keyword density and backlinking keywords to determine search engine rankings.

Meta Description – The meta description tag is one of the meta tags that are still used by search engines to display search results. This along with the title tag is used to display the name and description of the link on SERPs to the user searching for information.

Nofollow Links – Search engines spider the Web looking for information and in turn ranking the relevance of sites in its indexes. Nofollow links are an HTML attribute associated with hyper links that tell a search engine to not follow the link, stopping the search engine's traffic at that page, almost like a dead end. Nofollow links are optimal when it comes to making sure that your own page is optimized to the highest level possible by not allowing the link juice to pass through it.

Off-Site SEO – Off-Site SEO are the methods and practices of performing SEO work that happen away from the site itself. Off-Site SEO mainly involves the use of heavy backlinking, social media shares, authority site content creation (i.e. squidoo.com, youtube.com, etc.), article spinning, and so on. Off-Site SEO is a very labor-intensive part of the SEO trade.

On-Site SEO – Any work that is done on the Website to increase the effectiveness of its SEO is considered On-Site SEO. This includes any HTML work, content creation, internal linking, setup, keyword distribution, and other related efforts.

Page Title – The HTML page title is the descriptive site title detail that resides within the page's <title> tags. This information is displayed by the search engines and is used in ranking the site on the SERPs. A good page title tag should be descriptive but not superfluous and should accomplish its goal in around 70 characters (the cut off point for most SERPs) with the use of the primary keyword.

Pinging – Pinging is a technique that notifies the search engines to go out and seek data from a URL. This is required because a lot of the link building that is done happens on low, or no page rank sites that do not get visited often or at all by the search engines. When a search engine is pinged to go out and index a URL you can be certain that the hyperlink to your site or to another link in a link pyramid that's pointing to your site, will be found and indexed.

Panda – The Google Panda is a change in the algorithm for Google's search results that was released in February of 2011. The effects of Panda were to demote low quality sites and promote sites with high quality well researched information. The effects of this release were widespread, making huge shifts in positioning on SERPs forcing some businesses to lose large volumes of search traffic while others were able to gain it.

Page Rank – One of the most important descriptors of a Web page, the page rank is a Web page's rank in relevancy on the Internet, ranging from 0 to 10. Sites like Facebook, Twitter, and Google's home page achieve Page ranks of 9 and 10, while lower trafficked sites have lesser page ranks.

Penguin – The Google Penguin was one of the latest major updates released to Google's algorithm on April 24th, 2012, that began to demote visibility of listings on SERPs that violated Google's Webmaster guidelines and employed Black-Hat SEO tactics such as cloaking, keyword stuffing, and the creation of duplicate content.

PPC - Pay-per-click advertising, or PPC, is a form of paid search engine advertising that marketers use to get their message out to the masses on a large scale very quickly. PPC ads show up on the right side of SERPs and are now also being implemented on Facebook, YouTube videos, and more recently on sites like Twitter.

PPV – Pay per view ads, or PPV, is a type of advertising that is utilized by marketers to distribute ads to a user base that has expressly agreed to receive those ads. An example of this is free software downloads or online services such as Pandora that use PPV ads to display advertisements on a periodic basis while providing a free service.

Referrer String – Referrer strings are used in affiliate and Web marketing to pinpoint campaigns and where a lead or referral came from. This is important to some marketers running paid advertisements to be able to gauge the successes of their various efforts throughout the Web. Web programming dictates that after the Web page name, a question mark can indicate the start of any variables that may be appended to a URL, thus resulting in a Referrer String.

Robots.txt – This is a file that resides in the root directory of your Website, that provides instructions to search engines on any folders, or files that it shouldn't index. Most people don't want search engines seeing all files on their sites such as administration files, or other files that contain sensitive information.

RSS Feed – A Rich Site Summary (RSS) feed is a standardized format that allows for the automatic update and syndication of content on sites that have frequent changes and entries such as blogs and other news sites. The RSS feed format provides a standard in formatting that allows ease of redistribution of either full or summarized data, metadata and publishing information.

Sandbox – Google Sandbox Effect is an effect that happens when a newly formed domain name's link juice is not fully weighted due to filtering from Google in order to prevent SPAMMERS from reaching the first page in SERPs by registering multiple domain names quickly and actively promoting them.

Search Algorithm – A formula devised by brilliant minds that weighs and takes multiple factors into account when reaching a determination for search result page ranking. The Google search algorithm combines many factors including the aged domain factor, Website link popularity, On-Site SEO elements, and Off-Site SEO elements. No one outside of Google knows the exact current algorithm and the total weight of each of the factors that are taken into account or precisely how they impact search results but there are very good guidelines available.

SEM – SEM is the business of search engine marketing, the industry that search engine optimization specialists fall under. SEM is used to refer to not only SEO efforts but also paid search engine marketing efforts as well.

SERP – Search Engine Ranking Pages, also known as SERPs, are the end listing results pages of queries to search engines. SERPs will generally include a title and brief description of each listing related to the keywords searched along with a link to that content. In SEO the goal is to dominate the first page of SERPs.

Sitemap – A sitemap is a page that's created to aid browsers in crawling a site. A sitemap provides a hierarchical link structure of pages on a Website that are accessible and permissible to be crawled.

Social Media – Social media is a term that refers to the types of sites that have increased in popularity in the past several years that base themselves on end user interactions in a social and collaborative format. Examples of such popular sites are Facebook, Google Plus, and Twitter.

Spider – A Spider is a Web-robot that's instructed to go out and crawl the Internet for data used for the purposes of Website indexing and rankings. Google has multiple spiders that it sends out, some that are dedicated to deep-indexing the Web, others for more periodic updates to Web content, and even others for algorithm adjustments such as the Google Panda and Google Penguin.

Website Fold – The Website fold is the section of the Website that is viewable to the natural eye prior to getting cut off by the browser and forcing a user to scroll. The Website fold will vary from screen resolution to screen resolution, however it's typically 600 to 850 pixels down from the top of the browser.

White-Hat SEO – White-Hat SEO techniques are those that follow the rules and standards of the SEO world and also adhere to Google's Webmaster Guidelines. White-Hat SEO techniques, while more time intensive, offer the largest long-term gains for your Website's ranking on SERPs. These techniques include quality content creation, proper On-Site SEO configuration, and organically looking Off-Site SEO linking.